Railway Ties
1888–1920

Elizabeth Waterston

Rock's Mills Press

Published by
Rock's Mills Press
www.rocksmillspress.com

Copyright © 2020 by Elizabeth Waterston.
All rights reserved.

For information about this book, please contact the publisher at customer.service@rocksmillspress.com.

Contents

Railway Ties

Coupling / 1
Switch / 8
Sorting / 15
Changing Gauges / 22
Overpass / 28
Toronto West / 33
Spikes / 39
Timetables / 47
Signals / 55
Siding / 64
Strikes / 71
Wrecks / 79
Tracks / 87
Dynamite / 93
Junction / 101
Crossing / 108
Rails / 116
Tunnelling / 123
Locomotive / 131
Ballast / 138
Brakes / 145
Ties / 153
Concourse / 161

Afterword / 169
Illustrations / 170
Sources / 173

one

Coupling
Aurora, 1888

The story begins with a girl named Lizzie. No—a correction: she was called Lizzie, but her name was Sarah Christine Elizabeth, and she had been duly so christened in October 1867 at Trinity Anglican church in Aurora, Ontario. Lizzie was a Baldwin; her family owned the Baldwin Mills that stood down by the quiet river and the noisy new railway. The Baldwins still welcomed the plodding farm horses that brought wheat to the mill. But the fine flour they produced—the "Aurora Belle"—now went by freight train to the big Toronto markets. Lizzie's life would be tied to the railway, its signals and switches, its tracks and sidings. But she lived, for now, in the solid Baldwin house at the corner of Queen and Albert, in the small settled town of Aurora.

Lizzie was one of a family of five. She had two older brothers, Will and Howard, and a younger brother, Wyatt, and finally a sister, Anah Robena. Lizzie's brothers thought Anah was a funny little thing, toddling after them as she tried to follow them to school. Lizzie did not find Anah all that amusing. A hidden rivalry festered between the Baldwin sisters as they grew up. Lizzie collected a handful of roses from the front garden and made a posy for her mother. But little Anah was artistic; she painted a picture of the bouquet, more beautiful than the original flowers, and it was framed and hung in the parlour.

When they grew older, Anah's hair became soft and dark, like brown velvet. Lizzie's was brown too—"mousey-brown," the family called it. Lizzie saw a sharp-eyed grey-brown mouse emerge from under the kitchen stove and took a dislike to the comparison. By the time Lizzie turned seventeen, however, she had learned to rinse her hair with lemon juice, which brought out shiny lights and brightened the general

mousiness. Perhaps that was what caught the eye of a tall young man named Arthur Lloyd Smith, who asked her to marry him soon after they met in 1888.

The Baldwins were a bit alarmed. The Women's Auxiliary of Trinity Church had their doubts about Arthur, a newcomer to Aurora. He was only a telegrapher at the railway station. But a telegrapher's job, as Lizzie's mother explained to her friends in the Auxiliary, was sometimes the first step in a major career in the railway world. She quoted a story in the Aurora *Banner*: "William Van Horne, who just became the President of the Canadian Pacific Railway this year, began his career as a telegrapher in Illinois in 1857, at the age of fourteen." The ladies nodded. Everyone knew the name of Van Horne. A telegrapher might well be considered socially acceptable, after all.

Besides, it turned out that Arthur was the son of Major Lloyd Smith, the hero whose British regiment had joined Canadian militia going west to fight against the Riel Rebellion under General Middleton. Major Lloyd Smith and his men made history by travelling in an unorthodox manner. They boarded a pioneer westbound train. The Canadian Pacific Railway had not yet stretched to its final western point, and the line north of Lake Superior was still ragged, but the rails carried the soldiers as far as White River. Then they had marched over nine hundred miles toward Batoche, Saskatchewan, to surprise and defeat the rebels.

Major Lloyd Smith was still a famous hero. Since he had three other sons, he did not object when Arthur decided to work for the railway rather than pursue a military career. Now the Toronto militia kept the Major too busy to mind if the lad also decided to marry a Canadian girl. The Baldwins bristled on hearing this, but eventually agreed that the Major's son was an acceptable choice for their daughter. He and nineteen-year-old Lizzie became engaged early in 1888.

The busy Aurora station had already played its part in railway history. In the days when the Province of Ontario was still just a district called "Canada West," the first line of rail laid there had ended in Aurora. A wood-fired engine belonging to the Ontario, Simcoe and Huron Railroad puffed out from Toronto in 1853. This short line was named for two of the Great Lakes that bounded heartland Ontario on the south and west, and for a third small lake that led to the wilder northland. The OS&H railroad was familiarly known as "Oats, Straw and Hay," since its principal role was to carry farm produce to city stables—for the horses that were still the main engines of transport of Canadian goods and people. The OS&H had gone through a period of financial difficulty and was reorganized as the Northern Railway of Canada around the time Arthur first went to work. Then the Grand Trunk Railway acquired it, in this busy year of 1888.

Grand Trunk operations in Canada were led by an American named Charles Melville Hays. This was a little disturbing to Aurora hearts, which were still excited about Canada's emergence in 1867, confederated as a nation "from sea to sea." But then, William Van Horne was American-born, and so was Thomas Shaughnessy, and both of them were known to be prominent figures in the Canadian Pacific Railway,

the GTR's rival. Everyone knew that the GTR was gobbling up many small lines like the old Ontario, Simcoe and Huron, all part of its race against the CPR for national dominance. And yes, Aurora rail tracks now belonged to the Grand Trunk, and they continued proudly as far as North Bay.

Arthur Lloyd Smith worked in a station, erected as a showpiece for the GTR. The telegrapher's position was in a small bay, covered by a handsome gable roof. Arthur sat in the bay, coping with all incoming and outgoing messages that regulated movement along the mainline of the railway.

In the spring afternoons of 1888, Lizzie and Anah and their mother formed a habit of strolling down toward the river and then across to the Aurora station platform where they could wave greetings to Arthur as he worked. Ensconced behind the central window, one hand on the telegraph key, the other holding a bundle of paper slips, he translated each outgoing message into the rapid dots and dashes of Morse code—the only format that could be transmitted over the telegraph wires. He took a moment to wave back to his admiring audience, and then swiveled toward the big ledger where he had to record on the left-hand page in his neat legible hand the exact contents of each of those wired communications: "Messages Sent."

He then directed a second modest wave to the watching ladies. Lizzie responded enthusiastically, her mother graciously, and Anah languorously, having been pulled away from her easel to take part in this little family outing.

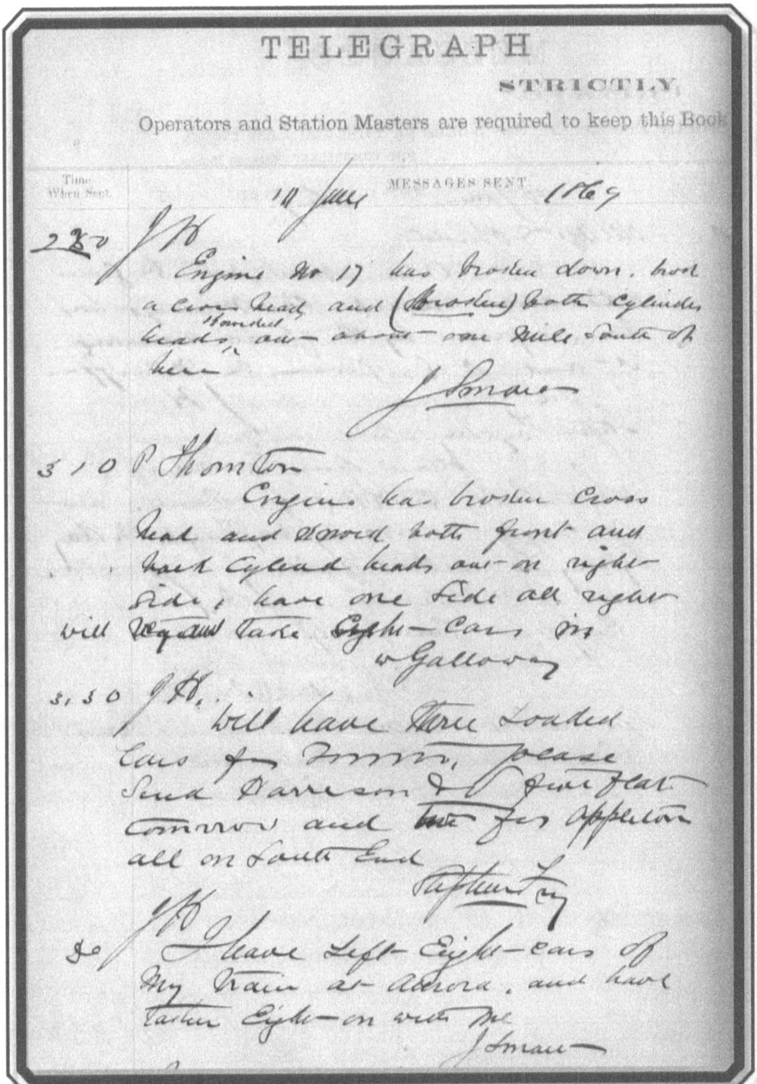

> **TELEGRAPH**
>
> **STRICTLY**
>
> Operators and Station Masters are required to keep this Book
>
> *[Handwritten telegraph log dated 10 June 1869 with messages recorded at times 2:30, 3:10, 3:30, and 30, signed by Smail and Thornton, concerning Engine No. 17 breaking down, broken cross heads, cylinder heads blown out, loaded cars, and cars left at Aurora.]*

Little did the ladies know that Arthur Smith was training himself to become, like the famous Van Horne, able to pick up on the messages directly, hearing the Morse clicks and simultaneously translating them into words and sentences. Now, as the office receiver became clamorous with dots and dashes, Arthur listened to the sounder and concentrated on that reverse form of translation, from Morse into English. Simultaneously he wrote what he heard on the right-hand page of the ledger, as "Messages Received." When the messages included orders to the train crews passing through the station, it was Arthur's job to copy them onto yellow slips, place them into a hoop fashioned something like a long-handled butterfly net, and pass them to the stationmaster, to be held up to the fireman in the train's engine, hooked by his arm, and duly read and obeyed.

In the evening, Arthur entertained Lizzie with snippets of news and gossip remembered from the day's messages—not, of course, including anything important pertaining to the Grand Trunk Railway's business. They arranged to be married in November, 1889.

The summer days passed, and wedding presents began to arrive. Lizzie's brothers Will and Howard boarded the train to Toronto, walked up Yonge Street as far as Ryrie's fashionable jewellery store, and ordered an engraved set of silver tableware. The monogrammed handles of the spoons and forks unfortunately read "LBS"—for "Lizzie Baldwin Smith." They had forgotten the baptismal "Elizabeth." (Lizzie hoped her future in-laws wouldn't notice.) Young Wyatt created a wooden breadboard for his sister. The Baldwin parents offered the young couple a handsome settee, a family treasure brought from Yorkshire two generations ago.

As for Anah, she painted a picture of a seascape with lots of frightening waves, beautifully rendered, and gave it to Lizzie and Arthur as her wedding present. Will and Howard carried it down Wellington Street, where Arthur had been assigned a small house, one of a row of railway workers' houses across from the railway station. This one was always assigned to the company telegrapher. Will hammered in a nail and carefully hung Anah's masterpiece over the vintage settee. Lizzie felt it better not to tell her family Arthur's worry: he got deathly seasick at the very thought of being on water. Arthur privately told her that he would sit on the settee with his back to the picture, looking out the front window toward the street.

Arthur suspected that the uneasy feelings between Anah and Lizzie were like the unharmonious relations between the various railway companies competing for dominance in Canada. A peaceable young man, he hoped that quieter days would come sometime, in both cases.

In the Baldwin family, Anah always outshone Lizzie. But once married and in her own home, Lizzie developed her own light. She added to the house on Wellington Street some "little elegant touches" suggested in the women's magazines such as *The Delineator*, *The Ladies' Own*, and *Butterick's*. A lace ruffle decorated the mantelpiece; a pewter vase inlaid with mother-of-pearl reflected the sunshine on the parlour window sill. As fall turned into winter, the flames flickering in the small marble-fronted fireplace and the lace ruffle fluttering above its mantle distracted the eye—Lizzie's eye, anyway—from Anah's picture of storm at sea. Lizzie fingered the carving at the back of the settee. "Do you like the look of the room, Arthur?"

Of course he did. He admired it sincerely. And when he sat on the settee and pulled Lizzie onto his knee (naughty fellow), they both rejoiced in the to-be-expected comfort (and the unexpected excitement) of married life.

two

Switch
Ingersoll, 1890–91

In January, 1890, the Canadian Pacific Railway Company offered telegrapher Arthur Lloyd Smith a chance to move to a better job. Was he willing to leave Aurora, and the Grand Trunk Railway, and step up into work as telegraph and railway agent in Ingersoll?  Aurora was a short distance north of Toronto; Ingersoll lay considerably west of Toronto—farther from the Baldwin family, and almost as far away as London in southwestern Ontario.

Like the Aurora station, the one in Ingersoll had a complicated history. The Credit Valley Railway had built it, and the Canadian Pacific Railway had taken it over just a year ago, when the CVR passed into CPR hands. Arthur would move into a station less fancy than the one in Aurora, but it looked tidy and dignified.

Lizzie remembered seeing in the *Illustrated News* a story about the Governor-General's visit to Ingersoll. Very grand, and in very good taste, she thought. She was willing to move; Arthur Lloyd Smith decided to switch from the Grand Trunk to the Canadian Pacific Railway.

The move to Ingersoll was to be the first in many changes in Arthur's career. He had entered the world of Canadian railways at a dynamic moment. Just five years earlier, the last spike had been driven into the transcontinental line of the Canadian Pacific. Out west, precursor lines proliferated, a network to be consolidated into the Canadian Northern Railway as the base of a second line across the continent. All across the country spur lines were tying towns, villages, and cities together in a new national political economy. Arthur was destined to shift many times from one part of the web of lines to another, tightening, connecting, regularizing. The move to Ingersoll would also be the first in a not-to-be-questioned series of changes in the lives of his wife and family.

As telegrapher and station agent, Arthur Smith would have to memorize the timetables of all freight and passenger trains passing through Ingersoll, in order to coordinate railway traffic between Toronto and St. Thomas. That Lake Erie town had been the end of the old Credit Valley line, and was still the connecting point for shipment to the Central Michigan Railroad. Working in Ingersoll would be different from work in Aurora; but Arthur felt ready to accept the challenge.

Lizzie, on the other hand, was not so sure of her ability to manage the move of her household goods. She could pack the silverware, china, linens, along with the mantelpiece ruffles and tea table doilies easily enough. But what about the bigger furniture—the elegant settee and the modest dining room set? Her brothers offered timely help. They would corral one of the big mill wagons, load all the household goods onto it, and turn the voyage from Aurora to Ingersoll into a tour for publicizing their excellent Aurora Belle flour. Will and Howard and Wyatt enjoyed painting "Baldwin Mill, Aurora" in large bright letters on the wagon side and making a jolly adventure out of the day-long trip down through Toronto and west to Ingersoll, with the big dray horses happily clomping through city streets and country roads.

"Our first move, Arthur!" Lizzie said with relief when all was unloaded into the Ingersoll house. Arthur's mind was too full of timetable schedules to do more than smile, shake hands with his brothers-in-law, and quickly slide back to the unfamiliar station that was his new domain.

On the south side of the river, the CPR station side, Ingersoll was still a quiet village set in a dairy farm county, a village of cheese mak-

ers, storekeepers, and retired farmers. But Ingersoll was changing, largely because of the railways. Newfangled factories sprouted on the far side of the Thames River, where the Grand Trunk had its railway line and its station and its new freight sheds. Ingersoll companies, such as Noxon's, maker of agricultural implements including mowers and binders, and Morrow's, producer of industrial screws, nuts and bolts, shipped their products by the GTR across the country. Arthur began to savour the atmosphere in Ingersoll, the sense of expansion from a strictly agriculture-based village into a town with different aspirations.

Lizzie's new neighbours in Ingersoll on the other hand were mostly a generation older than she was, and all of them were more conservative in taste. None of them was particularly interested in the young newcomer, so they left Lizzie to her housekeeping. She coped with the washtub, scrub board, wringer, and wooden clothespins on Mondays. On Tuesdays she coped less enthusiastically with Arthur's daily supply of white shirts, to be starched and ironed; Wednesday loomed with floor scrubbing and carpet sweeping—and so the weeks went on. But not easily. Lizzie was expecting a baby now, and not feeling particularly competent.

Arthur was healthier and happier. He enjoyed slipping into this unfamiliar community. He liked talking with waiting passengers. He also made a point of getting to know the railway's outside workers, the men who handled the work at the freight sheds, heaving heavy bundles and  boxes off and onto the freight trains. He developed a strong respect for the trainmen on local trains who had to hop down and shift the direction of the secondary rails so that their locomotive could haul its load onto the siding while the through train roared by. "You have to put your back into them switches," they told him. Most of the switchmen worked cheerfully, however; he enjoyed their stories of life on the line.

Old timers, though, told Arthur tales of earlier days and in particular the local legend about the mammoth Ingersoll cheese. Twenty-four years earlier, in 1866, Ingersoll people had collaborated in preparing a cheese that would compete in agricultural fairs. "It weighed seven thousand three hundred pounds!" a passenger waiting in the Ingersoll station told agent Smith.

Others in the small waiting room pitched in, "Six horses pulled the cheese to the old Great Western station here—right across the river. Then its case was tied down on a flatcar, carried by rail from here to Montreal, and on by ship to the Crystal Palace Exhibition  in London, England! We won prize after prize, and the cheese went by train all over Great Britain!" It was good to know that trains from Ingersoll had helped Canadian cheese reach cheese-lovers in the old country.

Those were the great days, they told Arthur, and James McIntyre, a local poet, became famous all over Canada as the Ingersoll Cheese Poet. They admitted, though, that the glory days of cheese were over for Oxford County. Cheese producers in other counties were getting ready to create new records for Canadian cheeses at the Chicago Columbian Exhibition planned for 1893. "But we've shifted attention to our newfangled factories." Arthur enjoyed the chats with people waiting for their trains. The station was a major social centre for the town: people dropped in for news and gossip as well as for catching and meeting the trains.

Lizzie perked up at Arthur's retelling of the cheese stories, but she was experiencing a difficult pregnancy now and felt less and less able to be cheerful, let alone able to cope with housework. She welcomed Arthur's parents, though, when they came for a visit from Toronto. They brought news, and a photo, of Arthur's brother Lincoln. He had gone to England, enlisted in his father's old regiment, and sailed to Africa to fight in the Boer War. "When he comes back, he plans to move out west to Vancouver," Major Smith told his astonished son and daughter-in-law. War seemed a long way from quiet Ingersoll.

As the months went by in the fall of 1890, Lizzie felt particularly unhappy about the Ingersoll doctor who made fun of her nervousness. Finally, in September, Arthur agreed to the Baldwins' urging that Lizzie go back to Aurora, where the doctor was an old friend, and her family could look after her until the baby was safely born.

Mother Baldwin enlisted her youngest son Wyatt to accompany her to Ingersoll to fetch Lizzie. They took the local Grand Trunk train from

Aurora to the North Parkdale GTR station. From there they crossed on foot over a series of tracks to the lofty Canadian Pacific Station (once the Credit Valley station) at Parkdale. The Canadian Pacific carried them westward to "Arthur's station." And there was Arthur, ready to welcome them for an overnight stay at the local hotel, the Kerwin Inn.

First, of course, they visited the little house near the Ingersoll station, and Mother Baldwin helped pack the things Lizzie would need in the next few weeks in Aurora before the baby arrived. Next morning, they helped poor Lizzie climb onto the conductor's stool and then up the steps into the eastbound train. Off she went, back to her parents' home, to be petted and cossetted during the last weeks of her pregnancy.

Arthur was almost too busy with the work at the station to feel lonely, but it was certainly strange to be alone at night in the little house. He sat on the elegant settee that had been the family's wedding present to him and Lizzie, and looked disconsolately at the disturbing waves in Anah's painting.

Late in September 1890, all concerns were allayed by the birth of a healthy baby girl. She was named Bertha for her mother's grandmother in Aurora, and Jane for her father's mother in Toronto.

Arthur took a short leave: Bertha Jane was to be baptized in the church where he and Lizzie were married. He travelled alone through Toronto to Aurora. Next day he brought his wife and baby daughter back home to Ingersoll.

Lizzie drifted through the first months of motherhood with little interest in envisioning the future for herself or her baby daughter. Back in Ingersoll she recovered her physical strength quite quickly, with Bertha Jane blissfully asleep in her new bassinet and Arthur delightedly watching over both of them.

Bertha Jane came into the world at a time when new possibilities were emerging for girls. Educational institutions were opening their rolls to young women, and consequently new opportunities in professions, previously exclusive to males, were on the female horizon. For Bertha Jane, however, the openness would be limited by the fact that her father was an ambitious, fast-rising railwayman. He would take his family with him into places lacking some of the opportunities of the brave new world of the twentieth century.

They had hardly settled into this new life before Arthur received an opportunity to unsettle it. His good work as agent in the Ingersoll station had caught the attention of his employers. He was approached with the offer of a major change. Was he willing to accept a station agent's position in the outskirts of Toronto, at the CPR station at

Weston, Ontario? The Canadian Pacific Railway Company had heard of the interest he took in the station workers. That was the kind of man they needed, to facilitate traffic through Weston itself, and also to react to changes in schedules and timetables arising as movement through the West Toronto sorting yard improved. They were prepared to give him a generous increase in salary.

Being close to Toronto seemed an even greater incentive for a move. It was a major city in Ontario and was also significantly closer to Aurora and Lizzie's family as well as to his own Toronto parents. Better seize the chance to move again, this time to switch to a more complicated and better-paid job. In 1891 the Smiths left Ingersoll and moved to Weston.

three

Sorting
Weston, 1891–93

Like every major city in Canada, Toronto had a big yard near its central rail stations, where engines and railway cars could be separated and reassembled between working trips. Like other cities, also, Toronto had several smaller sorting yards in its outskirts. Near Montreal, a village near Lachine was called, simply, "Sortin, Quebec." The major yard in the northwest area of Toronto in the 1890s was known as "The Junction." More and more incoming and outgoing rail lines crossed here, and the yard was continually enlarged. A growing number of trains dropped off some cars here and picked up others as they moved on to the north or to downtown Toronto and beyond. The rapidly expanding Canadian railway business necessitated rapid changes in the sorting process.

In nearby Weston, a village just west of Toronto's city limits, Arthur Lloyd Smith, the new Canadian Pacific Railway station agent, occupied a small office facing a simpler line of tracks. His primary work here would be similar to the tasks he had managed in Ingersoll: supervising the orderly running of trains into and out of Weston to the satisfaction of passengers.

A modest young man, Arthur was still surprised that the CPR had even been aware of his existence as an employee of their rival, the GTR. Even more surprising, however, were the directions his new employers now sent him. Besides doing the station agent's work at Weston, he was to get in touch with the yardmaster at the nearby Junction, keep track of current developments in the complex web of railway lines

there, and suggest to the Toronto office any consequent need for revisions in train schedules. An amazing order: he was to tinker with the sacrosanct CPR timetables! To a former telegrapher, focused on immutable times of train arrivals and departures, that sounded like heresy.

Nevertheless, after a few weeks of settling in to his new office and his new nearby home, Arthur prepared for a first visit to the neighbouring Junction. He arranged for a horse and buggy to convey him along the Weston Road to the point where a bridge lifted over the confusion of tracks. The CPR owned all these tracks, including lines that formerly belonged to the Toronto Grey & Bruce, the Credit Valley, and the Ontario & Quebec Railway companies. The Grand Trunk Railway lay close by, slightly farther to the east—but that was no longer his concern. He turned the rig down toward the yard and found his way to the yardmaster's office.

Station agent Smith introduced himself quietly, and then watched the ongoing work. Obviously extensive changes were indeed taking place here. The engineering department of the CPR in Montreal had recently sent diagrams showing a simplified pattern for proposed additions to the yard. A construction team had then moved into the Junction to implement the new plan and build a further series of receiving bays. Now, since the construction team had left, local labourers were beginning to handle rolling stock in the new configuration of tracks.

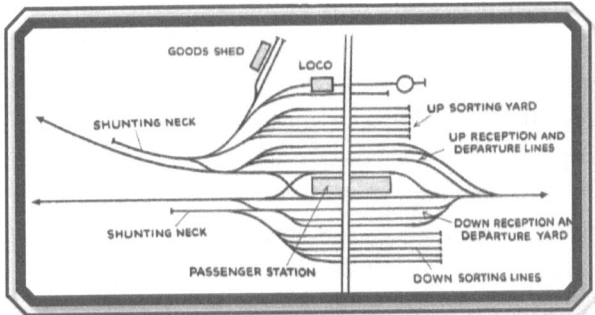

The sorting yard was a busy place, and a noisy place. Incoming engines pulled their cars into the new shunting neck and the uncoupling process began. Difficulties in uncoupling slowed the process at the outset. The old-fashioned "link-and-pin" units were heavy, awkward to handle quickly. Yard workers had to duck in between the two cars and physically pull the pin to unfasten these old couplings.

Small steam engines picked up and switched uncoupled cars—passenger cars or freight cars, for this was a "mixed yard"—into the newly built roll-in tracks, to stop at a buffer set at the end of each short spur. The sound of heavy cars jarring against the rigid buffers doubled the cacophony.

The small engines, familiarly known as "donkeys" then picked up the uncoupled cars, pulled them out of the sorting bays, and pushed them into new combinations with locomotives ready to leave the shunting area.

Arthur watched the action on the tracks, too deafened to ask many questions of the busy yardmaster. He realized with some trepidation how much he had to learn in the next few months.

Movement of trains through this augmented sorting yard would clearly cut time spent before the reassembled trains rolled on their way. Equally clearly that would indeed mean that timetables would need careful reworking to bring them into tune with the times.

Arthur drove back to Weston feeling he had at least taken a first step in understanding what he had seen. He must make sure that regular educational visits to the noisy Junction interlocked with the regular orderly days at his own station. And he must find time to make notes on possible changes in timetables, accounting for the changes that were roiling the Junction today and would increasingly appear in the near future. Today's trip had been a good start in a new life.

For Lizzie too, life in Weston began well. She was becoming more efficient at managing the indoor work of a young mother and housewife.

In the rather lonely afternoons she played dress-up with her pretty baby, expanding into experiments with couture. She had brought her mother's scrapbook with her—a gift to remind her of home. She did her best to adapt some of the stylish details pictured there. Bertha Jane became a model for testing new ideas about style. Since the Baldwins had always been dressed neatly, in durable sensible outfits, Lizzie kept quiet when she wrote to Aurora about her developing preference for lighter materials and elegant embellishments. For his part, Arthur thought Bertha Jane looked very fine in the new privately paraded styles of autumn, 1891.

On the first Sunday of each month, the young couple rode the local CPR train in to the Don Valley station in Toronto, then took a short walk south to visit Major Smith and Grandmother Jane. On the third Sundays, a different trip took them to Aurora. Lizzie was happy there, despite the small irritation of realizing that her sister Anah was not terribly interested in darling Bertha Jane.

In the busy days between these little jaunts, Arthur watched as more passenger and freight trains moved toward Weston station and on again. Like every agent in the district west of Toronto, he wrestled with ever-changing schedules as developments at the Junction sorting yards affected train movements.

On one of his weekly visits there, he was accompanied by a fellow CPR agent, the man in charge at Parkdale, closer to the heart of the city. This friendly middle-aged colleague had come over last November to introduce himself and offer a welcome to the district. Early in the new year he came again to see for himself the changes at the Junction that Arthur had described. Off they went together along the quiet Weston Road and down to the very unquiet Junction.

Train traffic here was obviously heavier day by day. Equally obvious were the changes in the daily processes. Early difficulties in uncoupling the railway cars, for example, were being alleviated. The old-fashioned link-and-pin units, heavy and so awkward and dangerous to handle, still joined many of the cars together. But many other cars were now equipped with the more modern "Janney knucklers."  These and other new devices for easier coupling and uncoupling meant a reduction of the number of accidents in yards all over North America. They also meant a speed-up in the change of directions by trains in the yard. Arthur mentioned to his friend and to the yardmaster that he had been reading reports of still lighter modern coupling equipment. He put in modest suggestions about new models that could be tested in the Junction yard.

The two visiting agents moved on to watch the uncoupled wagons as they rolled into the new short sorting tracks. They also rolled into a new series of difficulties. Buffers of different designs had been set up in the yard to stop the heavy wagons speeding in toward them. Each posed a particular problem for the yardmen who were charged with sorting and reassembling the trains.  Arthur queried the workers about which kind of buffer seemed to work best. The answers varied, but all workers reported the dangers inherent in releasing the cars at speed against any of the barriers.

Another newfangled idea could lessen these dangers, Arthur suspected. He told his fellow agent about a "hump" he had read about. A shallow hill had been built in some other yards, creating a gradient that would allow cars released at the top of the hump to roll down slowly under the force of gravity. This would smooth the impact of equipment rolling against the buffers. The yardmaster listened and promised to set some of his workers to build such a hump. The visitor from Parkdale expressed interest, though he advised that such a scheme needed many adjustments before it could be accepted.

Over the course of the next year, many such joint visits would recur, making a useful break in the steady maintenance of old-fashioned work at Weston, and an engaging opportunity for discussion of progressive ideas across the larger railway system.

Arthur Smith did not stay long enough in Weston to perfect his experiments, however. Once again, a change of jobs disrupted his busy work life, along with his home life and its smaller routines.

The Regional Superintendent had taken note of his observations about the sorting yard. Many difficulties remained there, but his superior assured him that time and new general regulations would straighten them out. The officials considered that even a young man as energetic and ingenious as A.L. Smith could not push his ideas for improvements in coupling and buffering and humping any further or faster. "Time will tell," the Superintendent said. He was, however, pleased with Smith's other work on timetables and on general maintenance of the station. "Now we want you to move on. You'll face a different set of problems at Woodbridge, and we're betting you'll clear them up for us. It's a nice little place, just a few miles north of here."

Arthur and Lizzie were going to be uprooted again. This time the presence of Bertha Jane would add to the stress of moving day. Arthur faced it as cheerfully as he could. He brought home two sturdy barrels, and asked, "Can you manage the packing, my dear?"

Lizzie assented, though feeling rather queasy. She was pregnant again and already she found it ever harder to cope with her household duties.

The work of packing indeed proved too much for her. Arthur sent a sad telegram to Aurora reporting a bitter disappointment in the hope for a second child. Lizzie had suffered a miscarriage.

Arthur wired an enquiry: could Grandma Baldwin look after Bertha Jane in Aurora, "just for a little while, so that Lizzie can recover strength and cope with the move to Woodbridge?"

Grandma assured him she was always willing to disrupt her home life in order to lessen her daughter's stress. She again enlisted Wyatt, now a sturdy teenager, for help on her journey. They took the Grand Trunk to Toronto and then the Canadian Pacific to Weston. Once again Arthur was there to meet them, this time with little Bertha all packed up and pretty, ready to take her first train ride.

In Aurora, Grandma petted Bertha, and showed her how to make pretty little arrangements of wild flowers on a small white tray. "Your Aunt Anah used to do this when she was a little girl," said Grandma. She had forgotten that it had been little Lizzie who was the flower arranger. Bertha's Uncle Howard and Uncle Wyatt were called on to play with her on Sundays after dinner. "This is the way the gentlemen ride," Wyatt chanted, bouncing her carefully on his bony young knee. Uncle Will had recently married a plump little lady named Mary, but on Sundays he brought her home for dinner at the big Baldwin house: another person to play with Bertha.

When Lizzie pulled herself together and sent for her little girl, the young uncles cheerfully boarded the train with her and made homecoming a happy game. Lizzie's spirits revived as she fussed over small Bertha and listened to Arthur's reports on his final day at the sorting yard.

He was winding up the odds and ends in Weston, leaving his ambitious plan for a yard hump in order, though he doubted that it would survive his leaving. He and Lizzie shared a hope that his work at Woodbridge would be less demanding, and that he would have more time in the evenings to help with the routines of parenthood.

four

Changing Gauges
Woodbridge, 1893

Woodbridge was a small village at the edge of Toronto, eight miles north of Weston, farther up the Humber River. The problem here was that narrow-gauge rail lines running through part of the village needed to be converted to standard gauge. The original tracks had been laid by the old Toronto, Grey & Bruce Railway. That was before the TG &B was acquired in 1882 by the Grand Trunk, which was better able to afford changing the gauge.  But in 1883, when the Grand Trunk went through one of its early periods of financial trouble, it sold the small railway to the Canadian Pacific. During these changes of ownership, a stretch of the line that lay near the Woodbridge station still remained in the old "narrow gauge" form. Its old cast-iron rails had been set with a mere three-foot six inches of space between them.

Other early railway companies in Ontario had built their lines at a "broad gauge" of five feet, six inches, also known in early days as  "provincial gauge" because it differed from the "standard" gauge, four feet, eight-and-a-half inches, prevailing in the United States. Rumour had it that this provincial gauge had been chosen to prevent American soldiers from roaring into Canada on "American" or "standard" gauge" rail. By the peaceful 1890s, the standard gauge had gained general acceptance in Canada, as in the United States.

Now, in the country near Woodbridge, new, more widely spaced rails had been set to replace the old narrow-gauge track. Only in the village itself, both narrow and standard lines remained in place in front of the station: a challenge waiting to be met. The long and complicated battle of the gauges had resulted in major problems for railway construction engineers, managers, and superintendents.

It posed lesser problems for a local station agent, such as Arthur Smith. The CPR found it expedient to send this trustworthy employee to keep the train service to the north and east going smoothly through the village while their work gangs realigned rails by the station.

Woodbridge was a pretty little town, its houses strung around the curves of the Humber River as it ran between the gentle hills northwest of Toronto. All these natural undulations, Arthur thought rather guiltily, seemed like the pretty curves of the young woman he had married. He shook his head and went back to a quick checkup of the workers who were re-laying the line, setting the wider-spaced rails in place in front of the station.

Shifting the new track into place was a familiar job for the gauge-change work team that had moved into the station area. They were hard at it, lifting and removing the old narrow-gauge rails and fixing and strengthening the placement of the broader new ones.

Even when the new section was in place, however, other workers would continue to face the heavy job of changing by hand the switches for opening and closing the line to the siding. Arthur believed that someday soon an electric wire would run from the station to a remotely controlled motor, placed near a new set of rods and

levers: a new kind of switch. In the foreseeable future, these levers would be electrically powered to change the points of track at a junction. Remotely controlled electric power would shift the levers, and the direction of each track would change as trains neared the station. The secondary track would be opened, to direct an eastbound train onto the siding, for instance, so that a westbound one could move toward the station platform and on again.

Railway work done by electricity: it was something to dream of in this new age of electrification. But Arthur was not sure he would be in Woodbridge to see such a change.

The friendly agent from nearby Parkdale came to pay a visit. He told Arthur, confidentially, that the Woodbridge appointment was probably just a stop-gap. The company was waiting for another post to fall empty. In fact, the man confided, it was his own present position in Parkdale that would soon fall vacant. "I am to move into the downtown executive offices, on King Street."

Arthur of course knew the Canadian Pacific Railway's business offices in Toronto. They were in a modest building dwarfed by the nearby Grand Trunk's Union Station. That handsome Italianate facility housed the Grand Trunk and also the Great Western and the Toronto & Nipissing railways. It dominated Front Street, and its web of rail lines stretched behind it toward Lake Ontario and eastward toward Kingston, Quebec, and the maritime provinces.

The Parkdale agent was undaunted by the present power of the Grand Trunk. "The CPR is in for a period of growth," he said. He suggested again that Arthur could probably look forward to holding a good position soon in the growing company.

Arthur decided not to mention this flattering speculation to Lizzie. She had found the move to Woodbridge exhausting. She was bravely organizing a new home again, and dealing with a rather demanding child. The promise of another move before too long would not appear propitious to her.

To cheer her up, Arthur arranged for Lizzie to have a photograph taken, holding her wide-eyed little daughter. Soon another formal photograph appeared, featuring Lizzie and her young cousin Gertrude Baldwin. Gertrude had come from Aurora on a long visit to help with the housework. She was young enough to restore the livelier spirits that had once charmed Aurora and captured Arthur's attention. Lizzie and Gertrude donned their best finery and posed for a picture together one Saturday, leaving Arthur in charge of Bertha Jane. He didn't tell the womenfolk that he found looking after a three-year-old was not quite as easy as he had expected. Fortunately, he liked the resultant portrait, and Lizzie's dress looked "splendid," he announced.

Soon, however, Lizzie had to abandon the tight-fitting dress. She was once again pregnant and feeling squeamish and uncomfortable. Young Gertrude promised to stay with her until the next baby arrived, though she was clearly innocent of any understanding of what the actual arrival might involve.

But in spite of Arthur's loving concern, Gertrude's cheering presence, and Lizzie's willingness to accept help and take her life more easily, the year in Woodbridge ended in yet another episode of painful loss. Lizzie endured a second miscarriage.

Within a very short time, Lizzie, worn out with weeping, had to listen as Arthur explained that they must face again the strain of moving. The Canadian Pacific Railway Company, his employer for the past four years, had offered him a significant promotion. Because of the excellent reputation he had earned already, he was to be appointed Despatcher (the traditional British spelling was maintained in Canada) at the bustling Parkdale Station in the west-central area of Toronto—a big-city job.

This news, so satisfying to him, was hard for Lizzie to adjust to. She was so troubled by the prospect of organizing and packing for another move right now that Arthur felt impelled to ask her parents if they could look after Bertha Jane in Aurora again—"Just for a little while."

The Baldwins' answer was hesitant. They had decided that their home was now too big for them, and were in the process of dividing it in two. Will and his Mary would move into the right-hand side of the house. They had converted the old dining room into a combination living and dining room, with the old kitchen remaining behind it. The big staircase still ran up from the entry hall, but the whole upstairs was also now Will and Mary's domain. It included a hopeful nursery and a small room for a nursemaid, "Just for the early days when Mary will need the most help."

Downstairs, a new door on the left of the big front hall now led to Grandma and Grandpa's smaller quarters. The old living room was now divided into their parlour and bedroom. Behind this lay a small guest room—and yes, that could be occupied by little Bertha during her visit. "That will be fine!" Grandma wrote.

In the large sunroom that spread across the back of the house, Anah set up her bedroom and studio. Here she had privacy, and a fine view of the big back gardens. Three-year-old Bertha's earliest memory would be of quiet times, standing in the Baldwin garden and waving to Aunt Anah. Anah would smile and wave, and turn back to her painting. She thought briefly of doing a portrait of Bertha but decided instead to finish a large oil painting of two rather menacing guard dogs, commissioned by their owner, an admiring neighbour.

Bertha, dimly aware of the indignity of being shipped between two households at incomprehensible intervals, asked incessantly, "When do Mother and Father come and get me?" Grandma's answer was a gentle "soon." But that "soon" ultimately stretched out over the better part of a year. In the interval, her parents underwent the stress of moving again, helped by dear young Gertrude.

In the late autumn of 1893, Arthur's stint in Woodbridge ended and he and Lizzie moved to Parkdale. He bought a house on Cowan Avenue, four blocks from the station, and hired some of the workmen at Woodbridge to manage the move of household goods from the small town to the major city. In railway terms, Arthur Lloyd Smith had "arrived."

five

Overpass
Parkdale, 1893–95

Parkdale, once an incorporated outlying village, had been annexed by Toronto in 1889. It was now flanked by new suburban growth to the west and north. A confusion of rail lines aiming at the heart of the city met here. First, the Canadian Pacific Railway, coming from the west, ran parallel to Queen Street, a major city thoroughfare. The CPR incorpo‑

rated some of the old tracks laid down by the Credit Valley Railway and the Toronto, Grey & Bruce line. The Des‑patcher's office provided a view of CPR tracks—and also of the rival lines of the Grand Trunk Railway.

From this office, Despatcher Smith could watch the two sets of trains chugging to and from the central stations farther downtown. Watch them—and worry. Just east of the stations the rails crossed Queen Street at Dufferin Street. Every level

crossing poses a hazard. This particular one, in‑volving Queen Street, a major Toronto artery, and a double track on the transcontinental path of the CPR, was doubly dangerous.

Adding further danger, electric streetcar lines had been laid along Queen Street recently. The old horse-drawn streetcars, though scheduled to be retired from service next year, intensified the immediate danger at rail crossings.

The good news was that negotiations had been underway for some time between the railway companies and municipal leaders. They had decided that the least expensive and least disruptive solution was to maintain the train tracks at ground level and redirect this portion of Queen Street into an underpass. A Queen Street underpass had been designed, to be dredged out a few blocks southeast of the Parkdale station, at Dufferin Street. Railway construction engineers were finalizing plans for building a double railway bridge over the dip that would be dug in Queen Street.

As Parkdale Despatcher, Arthur found himself sitting in on some of the current planning negotiations at Toronto City Hall or in the offices of the reeve and mayor in Parkdale. There he often found common ground with representatives of the Grand Trunk Railway, since the rival's train lines would share the overpass. After one meeting, the Grand Trunk's regional superintendent commented jovially, "You and I must stand together, Mr. Smith, against all these lawyers and politicians." Arthur smiled and agreed. The GTR man offered a small joke: the two railway companies were like sisters. "We are in competition, sure, and we feel jealous of each other. But we help each other out if things go wrong."

Arthur nodded sagely. The idea of friendly rivals appealed to his peaceable soul. Mutual help was a good way to do business.

He found a rather different version of rivalry at home. Lizzie had barely settled in before she wrote to her Aurora family to arrange for Bertha's return, and invite them to see her new house. Arthur suspected that Lizzie's reviving energy was being channeled into an effort to impress her family—and particularly her sister Anah—with her skill as a decorator.

Once again, Lizzie began to add "little touches" to the sunny rooms in the modern house on Cowan Street. They had chosen to live here partly because Arthur could get back and forth

from the CPR station easily, but partly also so that Lizzie could catch the electric streetcar at the corner of Cowan and Queen and go downtown to the big Toronto department stores. There she ordered delivery of the bits and pieces in the pretty, pale colours and the uncluttered turn-of-the-century style that was replacing the heavy darkness of late Victorian décor.

The whole Aurora family came to the pleasant Toronto suburb, bringing little Bertha with them. The elder Baldwins refrained from comment about Lizzie's newly decorated house. Toronto style, they felt, was a little prideful. But Howard and Wyatt, who had now moved out of the family home into bachelor quarters closer to the mill, enthused over the new light look. Finally Anah, as artistic authority, explained that Lizzie had achieved something in the pre-Raphaelite mode. Then she elaborated on "colonial aftermath"—the Canadian tendency to pick up styles years after they had faded in London.

Arthur noted the little rise in temperature that always accompanied any meeting between Lizzie and her sister. He recalled Mr. Johnston's comparison of the rivalry between the two great railways to the relations between sisters. But his new job kept him too busy to worry about either set of tensions. Now, as despatcher for the west Toronto district, he had to supervise the integration, week after week, month after month, as new minor lines were redirected into Parkdale when the Canadian Pacific Railway absorbed small local companies into its grand enterprise. He had to make sure that all the local trains, "which stop at every pump handle," arrived on time in central Toronto, after being shunted onto sidings when the great through trains roared past. Beside all this, he had to keep a close watch over the early stages of construction of the Queen Street underpass at Dufferin Avenue. The railway's reputation depended on the way construction of a bridge over the busy street and its streetcar lines progressed in 1894, as quietly and cleanly as possible.

Lizzie was glad to bring news of Arthur's important job and rising reputation when they visited his parents. Major and Mrs. Smith now lived in the east end of Toronto, beyond Jarvis Street. The family sat around the table for a formal tea. Lizzie found it hard to untangle Arthur's brothers: Lincoln, Charles, and the youngest, Harry Batoche— but which was which? She had barely met them four years ago at her wedding, and all seemed to have grown inches and moustaches since then. Arthur's oldest brother Lincoln had just announced his intention of going out west to Vancouver. Younger sister Natalie and mother-in-law Jane sat quietly, while the Major rapped out orders to the little maidservant: "More tea! On the double!"

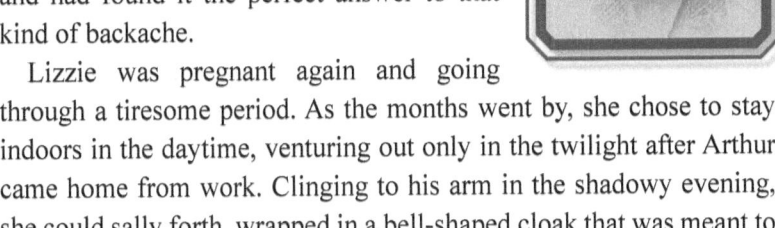

"Mother Smith" was kind, though. When Lizzie admitted to increasing back pains, her mother-in-law offered the loan of a particularly comfortable chair. Mrs. Smith had sat in it through eight pregnancies, she whispered, and had found it the perfect answer to that kind of backache.

Lizzie was pregnant again and going through a tiresome period. As the months went by, she chose to stay indoors in the daytime, venturing out only in the twilight after Arthur came home from work. Clinging to his arm in the shadowy evening, she could sally forth, wrapped in a bell-shaped cloak that was meant to hide her embarrassing shape. Perhaps the recurring family problem could be fixed. Lizzie's own mother was pleased to share her reviving hopes.

In March of 1895 a baby girl was safely born in Parkdale, given the name Zoë because that sounded so romantic, with the middle name Baldwin added because it seemed to suggest stability. But the baby was small and colicky, frankly not at all romantic, let alone stable. Soon it became evident that Zoë was a very difficult baby—not like the placid cooing scrap that Bertha had been. Her first six colicky months were so difficult that desperate measures appeared necessary. Arthur, worried about Lizzie's nervous state as well as about the baby's spasms, took it upon himself to write apologetically to Aurora. Knowing how fortunate he was to have this kind of a family, willing to bridge a difficult domestic situation, he asked if the Baldwins could look after Bertha, now aged five, until the time of stress was over.

The answer was a hesitant yes. Sadly, the big Baldwin home was no longer the happy place it had been. It whispered now with worry about Anah, who had not been well lately. A persistent cough suggested the frightening possibility that she might be in an early stage of tuberculosis. Nevertheless five-year-old Bertha would be welcomed, for as long as baby Zoë proved too much for Lizzie to manage.

Bertha found several second cousins exactly her age in Aurora. When September came and it was time for her to begin school, she was shielded from the teasing usually inflicted on newcomers by one of the cousins, named Eola Jaffray. Bertha found herself perched beside Eola at a high desk, confusedly listening to the other five-year-olds intoning "A cat sat on a mat." At the end of the puzzling school day Eola walked home with her. There Grandma helped Bertha assemble a new "posy show" so that she could sleep well and return refreshed to the funny marks that meant "cat."

Literate light eventually dawned, and Bertha learned to read (or at least to chant) "Get up, fat cat! Get up!" with the rest of the class. Grandma Baldwin was proud of her, though still rather irritated by the question, "Will Mother and Father come for me now that I can read?" repeated as autumn months slipped by.

In Toronto, Arthur Smith worried about Bertha's absence from her proper family, and coped with nervous Lizzie and colicky Zoë to the best of his ability. But he had to keep his attention clearly focused on work. And that work had changed again. Although he was still commissioned to keep an eye on the Parkdale construction of the overpass, he had now been promoted to a larger scale of management as Regional Despatcher for all of Toronto West.

six

Toronto West
1896-1900

Wrestling with the way railway cars moved through a succession of west-end stations, Arthur faced problems on a grander scale than he had managed before. He was charged to find and implement workaday 1896 solutions throughout his region. Timetable schedules changed here very often now, because of the ever-increasing number of passenger and freight trains moving through each station, to and from the downtown stations and larger yards. Arthur also faced constant requests for visits to the downtown office in the CPR building to take part in making major scheduling decisions.

At home on Cowan Avenue, Lizzie continued to make sure that Arthur had a good warm meal when he came home: leg of mutton, Irish stew, or shepherd's pie. She also made sure that he always had stiffly starched shirts and neatly darned socks. Mercifully, she now felt able to cope with the housework in the modern house on Cowan Street.

Lizzie and baby Zoë seemed to have reached a relatively stable state of health by late autumn, 1896. Arthur arranged to take time off from work in order to go up to Aurora to fetch little Bertha, just before Christmas. Grandma Baldwin bundled her into a red coat with a white ermine cape, new button boots, and a perky black hat with a red feather in its band. Anah painted her picture and said, "Goodbye, Little Miss Nuisance!" Then Bertha was kissed and hugged and told to be good by Grandma Baldwin and Grandpa, patted by the tall uncles Will and Howard and the now full-grown Uncle Wyatt, and placed carefully by her father onto a slippery caned seat in the railway car beside him, set to go "home."

In the small front hall of the house on Cowan Avenue, Arthur untangled her from her pretty coat and hat. Lizzie paced up and down in the parlour, with Zoë twisting in her arms. The baby, nine months old now, was at the moment red-faced from a furious crying spell. Lizzie had been nervous all morning and Zoë had picked up on her disturbance.

Bertha looked with distaste at the grizzling baby. Since Lizzie no longer had time or energy for playing dress-ups, Zoë was simply wrapped in a blanket, for ease of carrying through her colicky afternoons. "You take this one, Arthur—will you?" Lizzie cried.

Arthur lifted the baby out of her arms and fled to the back yard. Here were problems different from the ones he was used to sorting out at work. He paused, nervously holding Zoë, then paced the wintry yard in considerable puzzlement. Since he could manage an important job as a District Despatcher in the central city of Ontario, he felt he ought to be able to sort things out at home. Lizzie, back in the parlour, put on as welcoming a smile as she could muster for puzzled, pink-cheeked Bertha.

Arthur returned to work that afternoon, feeling guilty relief at leaving home. On the bigger scale of railway politics, he was concerned about a new strong threat to the Canadian Pacific Railway's domination in Canadian railroading. Charles Melville Hays, the ambitious general manager of the Grand Trunk Railway, was trying to convince Prime Minister Laurier that Canada needed a second transcontinental railway. Set slightly to the north of the CPR rails in western Canada, the proposed Grand Trunk Pacific line would probably end at a new terminal in Prince Rupert, B.C. Full-scale construction would not begin for a few years, but most people in the Canadian Pacific company felt uneasy about this surge in competition for continental travel and traffic. Arthur's responsibility was localized, but he was still in charge of the competitive movement of freight and passenger trains through an ever-enlarging city that played a major part in transcontinental business.

In 1897, he maintained a regular program of visits to the range of stations within his region, checking especially the efficiency of the ones

where a junction of lines demanded skill in interweaving local and through trains. He began by going by streetcar to the Islington Station in the southwest (an old station from the former Credit Valley line). Later he checked a small building at Emery near the corner of Weston Road and Finch. Though it was only a flag stop, he thought it might be in an area of potential growth.

He moved on to the more obviously important station at West Toronto. This was a transfer point for transcontinental travellers in 1897, since the city

did not yet have a central CPR station. Telegraph and telephone poles bristling near the station marked the innovations brought into Toronto through independent electrification companies. Here Arthur felt the new energy of a growing city and a strong railway enterprise.

His wife and young daughters, also full of new energy and enterprise, spent 1897 and then 1898 at home in Toronto, though not completely at peace. The tension relaxed a little when Bertha enrolled at Queen Victoria public school, a few blocks from Cowan Street. Though rather daunting in size, the school had a friendly and welcoming atmosphere. Bertha settled in and settled down. "We are managing very well indeed," Lizzie reported to her mother over

those two years in her weekly letters home to Aurora. On Sunday evenings she penned careful notes about little Zoë's improving health, and Bertha's readiness to learn how to sew—how sweetly her small hands folded hems on tea towels and wielded an uncertain needle through the layers of linen. "But Bertha tends to tease little Zoë," the weekly letter was forced to admit.

Lizzie pulled out the old leather-bound scrapbook she had brought from Aurora. Once an official Railway record book, salvaged long ago by Arthur when its official usefulness was over, it had been transformed into a receptacle for pictures of fashions, political cartoons, jokes, and poems. She showed her little daughters one of her favourite pictures: a stylish lady, happily supervising two well-dressed little girls as they played joyfully together. She hoped it would inspire similar harmony in Bertha and Zoë. That was the way sisterhood should be, she explained: "Birds in their little nest agree."

In Arthur's world, there was greater harmony. The Queen Street overpass, which Arthur had helped inaugurate, was near its successful conclusion. In spite of some minor miscalculations, four solid bridges, designed to carry trains of both the Canadian Pacific and the Grand Trunk in and out of central Toronto, now stretched over Queen Street. The two dominant railways had achieved an engineering feat cooperatively– a very important achievement.

Unfortunately, District Despatcher A.L. Smith would not be there for the public celebration of this visible sign of cooperative construction. Just as it began to be a peaceful place, the Smiths' little nest was destined to became again a movable one. Arthur had reached another turning point in his career.

Reviewing his work over the past few years, the management in the Toronto office had recognized a strong organizational ability. This efficient young man should betake himself (and his family, of course) for a short period to White River, near the north shore of Lake Superior. The Canadian Pacific believed this good organizer could improve efficiency at a troubled northern junction on the transcontinental line. Arthur's title in White River would be "Divisional Despatcher," a step up in the railway hierarchy. His superior officers assured him that he would be recalled to a new position in central Ontario as soon as possible.

Before telling Lizzie about this proposed move, Arthur consulted his father. He remembered Major Smith's stories about White River as an effective stopping point for his company of British soldiers in 1885, on the way to Manitoba to put down the Riel Rebellion. Major Smith, however, retrieved a memory of a cold, bleak place: not an enticing preview for the son about to relocate there.

Next, Arthur dropped in to the downtown CPR offices for more information. He asked about White River schools. The railway officials in Toronto assured him that there was a school, a very small one, but adequate. Rather disrupting for his daughters, young as they were, he felt, but the Company assured him that this assignment would not last long. As for housing, the Company would provide a modest furnished house. A minimum of household goods and chattels should be shipped north.

Arthur came home with these bits of information. Lizzie listened, in ominous silence. He assured her that the best way to protect "all her nice doodads" would be to leave them behind and shut up the Cowan Avenue house for the duration of his White River assignment. The Company agreed to pay for the next move after the White River assignment—whatever that assignment might be.

Nevertheless, Lizzie's lips tightened. Down came the trunks from the attic on Cowan Avenue and she began grimly to fill them with the minimum of essential items for life up north. Bertha helped fold and place the sheets, pillowslips, tablecloths, and napkins into the bottom of the first steamer trunk, protecting the layers with waterproof sheets, and topping them off with minimal pots and pans, baking sheets, and kitchen cutlery. Bertha and Zoë each chose a minimum of their playthings and added them to the trunk. Then they watched their mother fill the second trunk with blankets and pillows and comforters, and the final trunk with clothes: all the winter things brought out of mothballs in preparation for the early and long winter up north—hats and mitts and scarves and long underwear for all four members of the family.

Only after the girls were asleep could Lizzie wander around her Toronto house, touching the favourite bits of china deemed "not necessary": the turkey platter and soup tureen and the dessert plates, all gilt-touched, flower-decorated, and hand-painted ten years ago by gifted Anah.

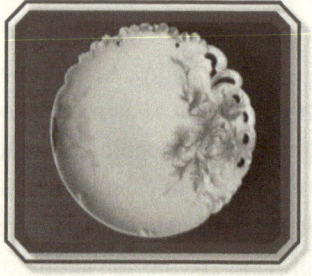

Late on the night before moving day Arthur shut and locked the big trunks. Workmen from the Parkdale station came in the morning to wrestle it all onto a cart and then off to the early train's baggage car. Away went all the treasures to White River. Away went the family, on to another new town, another new challenge.

seven

Spikes
White River, 1900

Arthur Lloyd Smith was moving into new responsibilities as Divisional Despatcher. At White River, he and his family were also moving to a new kind of landscape—a bleakness that they had never imagined in their years in southern Ontario. At first sight, a daunting place to make a new home.

For most Canadians, all the land that stretched north of Lake Superior was a region remote beyond imagination, set within the boreal forest, a wilderness world, cold and isolated. For the Canadian Pacific Railway, the region's wealth of lumber products promised infinite timber for railway ties and for the "timber corduroy" used for building across swamps. Another kind of wealth, not yet developed, lay beneath the surface of the district, just now being recognized as a huge mining resource of copper, cobalt, iron.

But the stretch of rail over which Despatcher Smith would have jurisdiction was not fully functional as a line to carry these kinds of natural resources to the major markets in Quebec, Manitoba, Ontario, British Columbia. Arthur was being sent to  unravel the problems currently besieging this stretch of the transcontinental railway.

The Canadian Pacific, in its ever-expanding web, was proud not just to build its railway but also to foster civic growth in remote areas of the nation. But White River, like so many of the places where the railway had established its new northern stations, still appeared in 1906 as little more than a dot on the map. The dot had been chosen in 1885 by Sir William Van Horne to become a divisional point on the east-west line. Ever since then, however, construction throughout the northern district near White River had presented harsh problems, including trouble with the railway workers.

Both passenger and freight trains experienced difficulties in traversing this area, because of interruptions of service. Crews trying to maintain the tracks were often halted by lack of essential construction materials. Contractors needed more ties, more rails, more spikes, more ballast, in order to perfect the line; but none of these could be delivered to the construction gangs without disturbing the regular scheduling of passenger and freight trains. The Company had sent Arthur, known as one of their most efficient despatchers, to straighten out these scheduling problems. The Canadian Pacific also expected him to produce detailed notes about the area, its people, and its natural resources.

The first view of the town of White River was not encouraging. The little settlement straggled around the curve of the river, alongside the railway. It boasted some forty families, augmented by a larger shifting population of railway workers maintaining the lines between White River and Chapleau to the east, and White River and Schreiber to the west. These trainmen spent the intervals between their

assignments in a big brick CPR boarding house. The family houses clustered near the railway station, a small unimposing structure to be replaced during Arthur's regime by something more permanent.

From the outset Arthur found the northern world friendly. The task of observing and reporting on available lumber and probable future traffic proved easy to manage.

He drew on his experience to begin improving the timetable system, establishing new train schedules of arrivals and departures, and wrestling a handy paper copy of the timetable through the local print shop. He organized a workforce to sort out the future positioning of rails in the complex patterns of the junction between various lines west, southeast, and northeast. Local boys came to work in the baggage room and in the ticket sales cage and to apprentice as telegraphers. The small station became neat and orderly, well adapted to the growing amount of freight and passenger business.

A.L. Smith was a quiet man, but he was very sure that the changes he was installing in the immediate area around White River area would improve the Canadian Pacific's efficiency. The men in the area work gangs accepted his air of assurance and cooperated cheerfully—not always the case in working relations in remote areas of the railway line. He moved through all these early stages in the rather cramped railway station and returned happily every evening to find out how Lizzie was managing in her own sphere.

The answer was "not very well." Lizzie and the girls simply endured a difficult sojourn at White River. None of them ever spoke about it in their later years. The great transcontinental line strengthened railway business through the north country, but that did not yet mean a quick northward spread of the kind of life to be found in southern Ontario towns like Weston or Woodbridge, let alone in a city like Toronto.

In the village of White River in 1900 many of the railway workers were unmarried. The Company maintained an adequate hostel near the station for their layovers. The small corps of wives lived in houses, across from the station, near the river. To Lizzie, their homes looked like little more than shanties. These women had no time for tea parties or afternoon chats about gardens or books or embroidery stitches. They had their own hard lives and their own worries to get through, with the help they could depend on from each other. They did not welcome the new Division Despatcher's well-dressed wife, who was known to be here only for a limited time. None of them realized—or cared—that they were not measuring up to Lizzie's standards. Poor things, they were having too hard a time simply keeping body and soul together in one of the coldest spots in Canada.

The men—the railway workers—seemed happy enough. Hammers clanged as the spikes fixed rails in new positions, improving the junction, making easier the way local traffic slipped into sidings as the transcontinental trains approached the White River stop.

Farther west along the line, contractors commissioned to improve the tunnels and bridges were less satisfied. One very tall man identifying himself as Harry McLean came to Arthur's little office to summarize specific problems and possible solutions. The materials needed for the work he had contracted to do were not coming quickly enough along the main line. Could his materials come instead by ship from Sault Ste. Marie, the port at the eastern end of Lake Superior? Good steel rails were available from the Algoma Steel company there. Alternatively, the rails, spikes, and stone ballast that he needed might come part way to White River from "the Soo" via the local Algoma Central Railway, which already ran from the north shore as far as Wawa. The CPR  ought to consider buying the smaller railway, Harry McLean said. That would give them an important link with the Lake Superior shipping offices and all the other facilities in Sault Ste. Marie: smelters, iron foundries, pulp and paper factory—all of them the creation of a fiery entrepreneur called Francis Clergue.

Arthur admired McLean's enterprise, and forwarded his suggestions to his superiors in the CPR's oligarchic headquarters in Montreal. He was proud to receive an assurance that McLean's idea of buying the Algoma Central would be carefully considered.

Lizzie could find no such pride in her domestic domain. She had no heart for trying to improve the drab little house that the Company had found for their despatcher. She survived by doggedly reading the fashion magazines that still came from Grandma Baldwin, *The Delineator* and *The Lady*. Lizzie grew as thin as the ladies pictured in those magazines.

Her two daughters also proved ill-adapted to White River. Ten-year-old Bertha was frightened by the mixed population of the one-room school, the hulking big boys at the back, and the small corps of teasing girls domineering over the newcomer. She had been as happy in her Toronto school as in her first school in Aurora, but here no kindly teacher or cousins eased her way. Lizzie went to the school to see whether she could help the overburdened teacher but was crossly dismissed as just making all the children act up worse than ever.

Under the circumstances, Lizzie and Arthur decided to keep Zoë at home, although she should have been ready to learn to read and write that year. Every morning Lizzie struggled to teach four-year-old Zoë her alphabet, then to fit in the housework so she would be free to read happy stories to Bertha every afternoon after school. Bertha tended to sniff sadly through the beginning of the readings, but she usually cheered up after a few minutes and enjoyed *Little Women* and *What Katy Did*. Zoë was less easy to amuse and to teach.

"It would be easier to show Zoë her letters if I had a blackboard like the ones in school," Lizzie told Arthur.

Ever the good manager, Arthur came home next day with a large blackboard under his arm. "It's a new one, just arrived by freight to replace the old one at the station. I told the baggage man I would just keep it for a few days; the old one is not too dilapidated."

The new one had gold lettering at the top: "Arrivals" and more gold lettering halfway down: "Departures." Lizzie drew a design in the top half

for Zoë: "Look Zoë, this is the letter 'k'. The letter 'k' is a tall lady" (she drew a loop high upward) "and she is picking up her skirt, just like a proper lady." The letter "k" looked elegant indeed on the upper half of the board. Lizzie went on, slipping the chalk down to the bottom half of the board: "Look, Zoë, the letter 'l'! The letter 'l' is a very tall man" (another high thin loop) "leaning forward and he has a little slipper with a turned-up toe in front of him!"

Before they could reach the letter "M," however, Arthur rather sadly returned the board to the station. The baggage man had reported that several people seemed to know that some station property had drifted into the despatcher's home. "You know how it is, Mr. Smith."

Arthur did of course know how it was. And he knew that White River was not working out well for his family, whatever advances he was making for the Company.

On Sunday, he took his two little daughters to watch the train from Kenora stop at the water tower. Very few passengers got off or on the train at White River, but every train had to take on water there. Arthur told the girls, "You can't have a steam engine without steam," and explained to them how coal fire in the engine turned water into steam to power the wheels to pull the train along. The girls smiled, uncomprehending but polite. "The boys at school put pennies on the track so that the wheels can pound them thin." Arthur smiled. "Thin pennies" were a treasured souvenir when he was a boy.

He stopped smiling when Bertha told him, "One boy is going to put a spike on the rail to see what happens." Horrors! Arthur's nightmares always exploded with train wrecks. He tried to calm himself by thinking of the White River workers pumping handcars along the tracks, checking for endangering debris. But he had better go to the school for a plain talk with those boys.

One of his main concerns was still facilitating the movement of construction materials into the area for the use of the CPR gangs completing intersections and  spur lines, as well as for the entrepreneurs such as Harry McLean, who had contracted with the CPR to strengthen tunnels and bridges in difficult stretches of the main line to the east.

For himself, though this rough life was alien to his quiet nature, he enjoyed hearing the tall tales of McLean and others when they dropped into his office to say hello, and swap stories about punching out tunnels and fling-  ing up bridges. Sometimes Harry brought along his friend Dan Hillman, a sturdy CPR surveyor, considerably less tall than Harry, but

 doing work just as essential to the Company's future. Dan was just back from a fall sortie into the wild woodland north of White River. The Company had to know how much good lumber grew there, and how much difficulty the terrain would offer when the time came to haul out the great trees and send them away for finishing into railway ties. Now that Dan's survey was completed, he was directed to draw up engineering designs for the work that Harry's men would turn to next.

Arthur relished the conversation of these two men, both a little younger than himself. One time, when they had come to White River to pick up supplies, he brought them home for dinner. Since they would be spending the night in the trainmen's bunkhouse, a homestyle dinner sounded wonderful. Lizzie laughed at the men's quick wit and graphic stories. Dan told of his recent life on survey, when he spent his days in rough terrain, accompanied only by a native guide and assistant; Harry added livelier stories of fights and pranks among the men on his construction gang. Lizzie packed off the little girls early to bed and stayed as an eager listener while the men traded railway talk.

That turned out to be one bright spot in a lonely time. The other consolation during the White River sojourn was that the two little girls hardly had the energy to squabble. Lizzie emphasized this good news in her letters to Aurora.

But the return letters from her mother further darkened Lizzie's moods. In spring came the bad news that Anah was showing dangerous signs of advanced tuberculosis. All the old antagonism faded in Lizzie's heart as she struggled to write consoling and hopeful words to her mother. Bad turned into worse: Anah's health rapidly deteriorated, and within mere months came the distressing news of the death of the young woman with such artistic promise. The difficulties of arranging train travel meant that Lizzie could not even go to her old home for Anah's funeral, to try to console her parents and brothers.

At the end of a dreary year, Arthur heard from the head-office people that he and his family were now to move back south. His work up north was considered successfully completed. He would return as Chief Despatcher for the whole Toronto Region.

When they first arrived, Arthur took Lizzie and the little girls out for dinner in the old Walker House hotel on Front Street: a memorable outing. All would remember the feast of roast beef and Yorkshire pudding for many years. "Very pleasant, Arthur," Lizzie smiled at him—the first smile for some time. She was back in Toronto. Back in civilization.

"Yes, Mother. Very nice indeed." Arthur had given up calling her "Lizzie." It seemed easier to chime in with the way the two young girls addressed her. They might as well all call this quiet, hard-working person "Mother," he thought. Or maybe he didn't think; maybe he just slid into the habit of reassigning an appropriate name to his helpmate, admirer, and co-worker.

eight

Timetables
Toronto, 1902–04

As they settled into the Cowan Avenue house again in 1902, Lizzie and Arthur began to feel more closely connected with their old Toronto neighbourhood. They joined the regular congregation at nearby St. Mark's Anglican Church at the corner of Cowan and Queen. Arthur found the slow Sunday rituals a welcome relief from the incessant emphasis on time in his weekday life. Every CPR station boasted an oak-framed clock, bearing the name of the company  and reminding everyone that this system prided itself on rigid accuracy in times of arrivals, departures, and connections. Arthur relished that imperious pressure of his timetables, but found satisfaction in occasionally slipping away from them.

Lizzie enjoyed being back with like-minded people. On her second Sunday at the church, three ladies of the congregation invited her to join them next day for a shopping trip to Eaton's and Simpson's department stores. Being in a city that was part of the British Empire had its fashion advantages. American ladies often came across the Canadian border to finger and buy tweeds  from Scotland, linens from Ireland, and Liberty cottons from England. Lizzie delighted in the thought of bringing herself up-to-date. She could buy some of these fine fabrics and copy the styles featured in the new Eaton's 1902 catalogue. She would not feel outshone by her new friends in their "boughten" outfits.

Much as he enjoyed seeing Lizzie's restoration to happiness, Arthur often drifted into abstraction while she talked the fashion talk. He was adjusting into his new duties as Chief Despatcher of the entire Toronto region. He began his tenure by visiting some of the stations newly under his supervision. The busy, sprawling North Toronto Station, set in a midtown area less familiar to him, was now the major stop in central Toronto for most Canadian Pacific trains. In contrast, the little station near the Don River was surrounded by yards awash with mud while tracks were being laid again.

Whether in the big station or the small one, Arthur needed to urge the personnel to recognize the significant changes in railway movement in and out of the city. He informed them that timetables were being constantly updated, to match the rapid changes around Toronto: the acquisitions by the CPR of smaller companies, and the

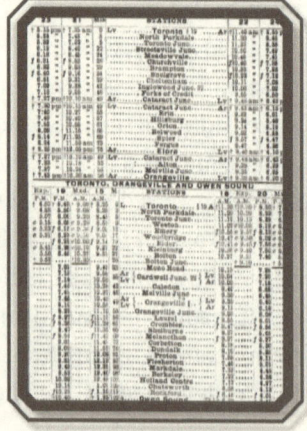

realignment of secondary lines to conform with the rise and fall of local manufacturing concerns. He reminded the local station staffs—agents, telegraphers, baggage handlers, and freight managers—of imminent improvement in communication between the stations. Whereas the current timetables for railway patrons had developed through long-ago personal exchanges within each small railway line, all new changes could be easily accessed and reproduced through the new telephones. Station agents would be able to offer their customers up-to-date timetables, reflecting changes in the rapidly developing city and province.

As a former telegrapher, Arthur testified to the coming of a new age of electrification at surprising speed. But the fact that his old specialty had virtually disappeared made many of his listeners uneasy. Would the vaunted electrification cut out other jobs now done by hand? He found the indoor employees less interested in discussing the effect of coming electrification on future scheduling and timetables, and more interested in present uncertainties about their own work if centralization reduced the importance of smaller stations.

Speaking to the yardmen at each station, Arthur promised speedier and safer switching of trains onto sidings, again through electrification. Even with a richer flow of traffic, and more coupling and uncoupling in the yards, electrification would ease their work. Again, he met uneasiness about these changes in the yards. The workers alerted him to the fact that such questions were being mulled over unfavourably by city-wide labour unions.

The Canadian Pacific Railway Company management had little sympathy with the current union movement. Arthur, however, was somewhat opposed to his company's stance. He had seen the underpaid, undervalued work gangs in White River. Now in the Toronto sorting yards he saw recent immigrants, unable to understand orders given in English, yet handling essential equipment, and old-timers who resented the newcomers' presence.

Somehow the railway workers in and around Toronto stations became aware of his understanding and sympathy. At least partly as a result, pilfering and vandalism lessened in his jurisdiction. The Company management approved of this reduction, even if they would not have approved of the hidden source of the change. Arthur maintained a quiet demeanour but he was increasingly worried about the right way to help the workers without endangering his present position.

Lizzie could not share his concerns. She was determined to be happy now that she was back in Toronto. She was finding friends. Mrs. Struthers, wife of the local doctor and mother of a very large number of children, was at hand to offer advice on any imaginable family problem.

The only fly in the Toronto ointment was the tendency of Bertha and Zoë to bicker about every possible topic. Once Lizzie sent the two girls around the corner to play in the nearby Queen Victoria Public School yard. Zoë soon trailed back soon in Bertha's wake. "Bertha drags me—DRAGS ME—I can't keep up!"

"Tell-tale-tit!" Furious Bertha hurled the schoolyard taunt and completed it: "Your tongue shall be split!"

"Good heavens, Bertha!" Lizzie cried, "Where did you hear that?"

"White River," Bertha said as she flounced away.

Lizzie no longer thought of her daughters as birds in a little nest, but as snakes in a pit. The girls seemed to twist everything into recriminations and huffs. "They'll grow out of it," Arthur said mildly after a dual exhibition of temper and grievance. He watched in bewilderment: these problems were beyond his managerial gifts.

The end of summer brought a surprising peace between the girls as they settled into the established and binding timetables of Ontario schooling. Zoë, enrolled in the second grade at Queen Victoria School, was at first so intimidated that she ran home from school every day at recess. Bertha, to her parents' surprise, took it upon herself to comfort and cheer her little sister and helped her settle down. As the weather grew colder, Zoë decided it was more fun at school than at home, so she abandoned the runaway practice.

Bertha, enrolled in the grandeur of the Parkdale Collegiate Institute, was shy at first. Her memory of being repulsed as a "new girl" in White River was still painful. Luckily, the Struthers girls helped her find her way around, and convinced her that a little sister was not an unbearable burden.

Just before Christmas a sad telegram arrived from Aurora to disturb the Smiths' peace. This time it was Grandpa who wrote.

Could Lizzie "come home" for a little while? Grandpa was frightened by Grandma's deep and continuing distress about the loss of Anah. Lizzie decided she must go, and she would take Zoë with her. Bertha and Arthur would have to struggle along alone, even though she might be gone over Christmas.

Arthur was almost too busy to notice her absence. He took Bertha to the Walker Hotel for a gala Christmas dinner, led her on a pleasant walk around the downtown Toronto area, showed her, with pride, the Grand Trunk Union Station where he occasionally attended a meeting nowadays, and then went back to work.

The threat of labour disruption was intensifying in central Toronto. In the United States, the American Federation of Labor was threatening a series of major strikes. Toronto, so close to the nation across Lake Ontario, shared the American expectation that such strikes were imminent. A Trade and Labour Council had been established in Sarnia the previous year, an early example of amalgamation of various trade unions in Canada. For the Brotherhood of Railway Trainmen, organized in the 1880s, the new general council strengthened hopes of getting responses to their demands for better wages, shorter hours, and overtime pay.

Arthur was unusually sombre when Lizzie returned from her own sad time in Aurora, worrying about her parents. But Zoë, bustling in behind her mother, managed to lighten the atmosphere in the house. She had enjoyed a fine time in Aurora. Grandma had found comfort in petting her; Uncle Will and Aunt Mary had set her to play with their baby boy Gordon; and the bachelor uncles Howard and Wyatt had let her roam around the old family mill and enjoyed answering her sharp questions about its workings. She came back to Toronto, eager to return happily to school.

Bertha, sleek with self-esteem in the wake of "running the house" while her mother was away, was even happier when the principal of Parkdale Collegiate reassessed her abilities and advanced her into second year. A teacher discovered that she had a flair for writing. Most of her stories were about life in a benighted backward village in the distant north. Both teacher and schoolmates relished a rather superior feeling as they chuckled over Bertha's light ironic touch in the tales of

White River. At the end of the 1903 school year, she was awarded a school pin for her work in editing the school paper.

Arthur bought a piano as a reward for the girls' progress and found a music teacher among his new acquaintances at St. Mark's Church. Zoë took to playing with fervour, but Bertha practised with more regularity.

It was a strain to find time for such involvements in his daughters' affairs, however. His job as Chief Despatcher involved ever more responsibilities. Rail traffic was growing at an almost uncontrollable pace and the lack of a major central station to integrate Canadian Pacific business proved more and more troubling.

In April 1904, the terrible "Great Toronto Fire" had razed the east-central part of the city. The Grand Trunk's Union Station survived,  just out of range of the devastation. Its Italianate towers still loomed through the smoke as one looked west along Front Street from Bay Street. Arthur heard speculation that a new enlarged Union Station might be developed by the Grand Trunk Railway on the burned-out area.

Partly as a consequence of the fire, there was serious talk later in 1904 about converting the handsome old building into a real "Union Station," harbouring the Canadian Pacific Railway as well as the Grand Trunk and its various affiliate lines. Negotiations were difficult. The Grand Trunk had antagonized the Canadian Pacific by initiating its own transcontinental line in 1902, with Laurier's approval. Canadian Pacific people muttered, "Why would Canada need two lines, especially when each cost so much in construction and maintenance—and when both already faced so many problems with the labour force?"

The atmosphere was not right for talking of turning the Grand Trunk's so-called Union Station into a place of genuine union, housing tracks of both Canadian Pacific and Grand Trunk trains. Yet in spite of the mutual distrust and hostility, the managers of the two giant companies began devising tentative plans for just such a Toronto Union Station. Surely someday CPR passenger trains could share the Union Station platforms with the Grand Trunk trains.

Years might pass before the architects' designs for a new terminal were approved and construction of the building and its viaduct could begin. Nevertheless, the planning went on, and Arthur Smith had a chance to play a part in the initial stages. In 1904, as Chief Despatcher, he helped all CPR station agents draw up possible timetables for an impending amalgamation, pinpointing necessary changes in train schedules. He also helped draft new procedures in all outlying areas so that Toronto could remain free from accidents as it emerged as a new focal point of all freight and passenger service in Canada.

Once again, he made the rounds of the stations under his direction. To the outside workers labouring in the switching yards and at the junctions, he prophesied that electricity would again bring important changes. The Grand Trunk, he told them, was already using telephones instead of call boys to carry messages around its new Mimico yard. Once again, he was met with a rejection of his assumption that labourers would be delighted with the new regime or advantaged by the so-called progress.

CPR employees working in the yards at local stations raised more urgent questions concerning their own working conditions and the "perks" they were accustomed to. Many men at the lower level of employment had been guaranteed pensions. Many, like Arthur himself in his earliest days, held the right to a house near the station. Would these conditions continue to apply, as changes in the railway system were implemented? New advances in communication had also allowed labour organizers to stir awareness of looming problems.

At his monthly appointments with downtown CPR executives, Chief Despatcher A.L. Smith could at least reassure his superiors that personnel at all western and northern Toronto stations were working well at present. He moved quietly through meetings, helping the transition to a new kind of centralization. In his own vision of the future, all the existing trains—Canadian Pacific and Grand Trunk, along with the remains of older small lines, the Northern Railway of Canada, the Great Western, the Credit Valley—would soon run safely in and out and through Toronto, thanks to the good work of all employees, and the grace of God. His comments were well received.

As he walked home to the house on Cowan Street, it struck him that it was like a railway station too, with its yard at the back and its platform (verandah) at the front. And Lizzie, dear Lizzie, acting in her station in life as baggage handler, yard manager, cleaning staff, cashier, and signaller. She was as successful at her work as he was in his. He was glad to inform her of his current success.

Ironically, from Lizzie's point of view, this kind of success led to another familiar, dreaded moment. The Smiths were destined to move on again.

"We are concerned about a situation in southwestern Ontario," the Divisional Superintendent told him. The Canadian Pacific Railway Company was losing business to the Grand Trunk there because of the rival company's connections with Detroit and Chicago. The CPR needed someone in London with communication skills, to sway businesses and politicians to work with it. The company believed that A.L. Smith could succeed in preserving the CPR's lead in the area. He would face a problem, not in labour, but in public relations.

Arthur left the office and went home to Lizzie with news that yet another move was in the offing. This time Lizzie cried, "We have moved six times now, in fourteen years of marriage, Arthur." Tears welled. "I cannot believe you expect me to pull up stakes again!" But it was true. Arthur had been reassigned to London, Ontario.

nine

Signals
London, 1905–07

Lizzie's despair was unwarranted. The years in London proved to be a turning point to happiness for the whole family. For Chief Despatcher Arthur Smith, the CPR Station in London that would house his office held obvious charm. With its neat gardens and ample platforms, it was an efficient workspace for Arthur and his men. He took particular delight in the modern signal box, lifted high above the tracks, clearly visible to incoming trains.

From the days of his literally hands-on telegraphy by Morse code, Arthur had watched the changing use of semaphore apparatus, at first consisting of movable wooden arms connected to upright poles beside the railway tracks. The position and colour of those arms had sent oncoming traffic messages such as "the line ahead is clear" and "switches are set correctly," and conveyed orders to proceed at a given speed, or to pick up new orders at the next station. Once operated manually by means of rodding, or with wires and pulleys, the semaphore arms at the very large centres such as Toronto had gradually shifted to electric power, giving operators there a better control over the movement of trains.

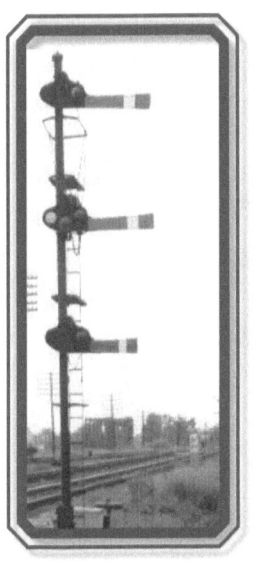

55

By 1904, railways all over the world accepted yet another major change in signals. Electric light bulbs developed by Westinghouse began to replace the kerosene oil lamps that had to be lit by hand every evening. Now, behind the coloured glass "spectacles" mounted on the painted semaphore arms, electric bulbs made the red, yellow, or green lights shine more brightly in the dark. Arthur, as Chief Despatcher newly in charge in the London district in 1905, ordered the installation of some of these electrically illuminated signals for use in the area, restricted to trains moving at low speed. He took pleasure in seeing London move to the forefront of international change.

As for Lizzie, in London she at last had a house she loved. Arthur admitted that the small house on Cowan Avenue had been unexciting ("charmless" was Lizzie's verdict—and incapable of becoming charm-

ing). The yellow brick house Arthur bought on Talbot Street was nicely proportioned and boasted stained glass windows on the stairwell and in the front living room. They had hardly enough furniture to fill the handsome front parlour. There was a tiled bathroom upstairs. (Lizzie shuddered when she thought of the White River outhouse.) Downstairs a modern kitchen had a handy pass-through to the panelled dining room. With the girls' help Lizzie unpacked some of Anah's beautifully hand-painted dishes and set them on the plate rail at the top of the dark panelling. Anah's seascape, that long-ago unwelcome wedding present, could be safely consigned to a dark corner in the upstairs hall.

Arthur returned happily to his own workplace in the Canadian Pacific Station, at an easy walking distance from the Talbot Street house. The Station was clearly less glamorous than the Grand Trunk Station some eight blocks south—one of the substantial and elegant stations built to Sir Casimir Gzowski's specifications to emphasize the good taste as well as the power of the Grand Trunk Railway. Arthur made

a point of meeting the man who was his opposite number in the Grand Trunk and establishing friendly relations with him.

But A.L. Smith had not been sent to this southwestern corner of the province of Ontario to be friends with the Grand Trunk. The two companies were locked in rivalry for control of the approach by rail to American markets. Both ran trains from London to Windsor, but the Canadian Pacific's only option was to transfer goods and passengers onto a Windsor ferry to cross the St. Clair River to Detroit. The Grand Trunk, however, had an additional and far more economical option of crossing into the United States. They moved freight through a single-track tunnel from Sarnia to Port Huron and onward to Chicago and the western states. Arthur soon decided there was little he could do about that—and in his British-Canadian heart he was not overeager to expand the Canadian Pacific Railway into a Pan-American enterprise. But looking toward north and east, toward Sarnia, Hamilton, Berlin, and Toronto, he could see more hope of expanding CPR business and outpacing the GTR for markets and resources in southwestern Ontario. At the end of his first week in London, he walked home, puzzling over the right way to help the CPR capitalize on its regional connections.

By chance, the position of his new house on Talbot Street helped solve this problem. It stood right across from the grand mansion of Sir John Carling. Not only was the Carling brewery London's major employer, but Sir John had gone on from brewing into politics and represented London in the federal Parliament for three successive and successful terms. He was a philanthropist and an organizer of friends and neighbours into similar philanthropic efforts.  Gossip at the station suggested that as well as running his very profitable brewery, Sir John was deeply interested in the development of London as a major rail centre. In earlier days he had induced several small lines to run through the city and had used his influence to entice the Grand Trunk to manufacture their train cars in London. Obviously, Arthur, as the new representative of the Canadian Pacific, should consult his distinguished neighbour about ways to strengthen the company's presence in London, relative to the ambitious growing power of the rival Grand Trunk.

Fortunately, Carling's wife was ready to welcome newcomers to Talbot Street. She explained to the ladies invited for tea to meet Lizzie, their new neighbour, "Dear John will be here soon. Just like a man," she chuckled, as if she were speaking of an ordinary husband and not the famed Sir John Carling. "Always late for everything. But I suppose all men are the same. No sense of time!"

Lizzie, being the guest of honour at this afternoon tea, concurred. She felt a slight twinge of guilt as the thought of always-on-time Arthur crossed her mind, but she decided that Lady Carling was probably right in general. "Lucky for them they have us," she laughed.

Lady Carling laughed too. "And we are lucky they need us, my dear!" Lizzie felt lucky that Arthur's work had taken her to this pretty parlour in this grand house on this respectable street in this prosperous and friendly small city. She happily answered questions about her young daughters and accepted advice about their schooling: nearby Talbot Street School for ten-year-old Zoë, and Miss Murray's private academy for Bertha, the fifteen-year-old.

Arthur was delighted to think that his little Lizzie had been accepted into the circle of the Carlings. He hoped he would be equally fortunate in forming a friendly bond with Sir John someday soon. The girls picked up on the general happiness and sat neatly in their places, trying to look like the proper daughters of such well-connected parents.

Arthur worried, however, at thought of Miss Murray's Academy. "A private school?" Lizzie agreed that it might be expensive, but in the end Arthur weighed the cost of a private school against the social value of following Lady Carling's advice.

No one asked for Bertha's opinion, let alone Zoë's. Zoë piped up anyway. "I'd rather go to the same school as Bertha."

Lizzie was ready for that. "Miss Murray only takes girls from twelve years old and up. You must wait your turn, Zoë." Arthur realized that the decision seemed to have been made while he was still considering it. He nodded one last time and voiced the obvious truth: "Then it's all settled."

A week later Lizzie went with Mrs. Macarthur, one of the ladies who had been at Lady Carling's tea party, on a little shopping expedition to Kingsmill's excellent store, right around the corner at Talbot and Dundas. The day was so breezy that both women fastened their hats firmly, wielding long wicked-looking hatpins. Both ladies were looking to buy new hats, perhaps like the black velvet model in the new Eaton's  catalogue. The two women discovered that they shared frustrations over the ways of adolescent daughters.

A letter from her own mother was waiting when Lizzie reached home. Grandma Baldwin was planning to turn part of her house over to Will and his wife Mary. She must empty the living room, in order to make a space for Mary's dining room set. And so—and so, could Lizzie and Arthur find room in their big London house for the parlour set that had been in the family so long? Another delight! The occasional chairs, with their elegantly carved backs, could be grouped, artistically, to form a conversation circle with the Victorian sofa, under the big bay window. The old wedding-present settee would be relegated to the small den. When the parlour set arrived by freight from Aurora, it fitted in perfectly in Lizzie's eyes.

Arthur was pleased to agree. He was even more delighted when a short time later Sir John Carling offered to meet and discuss with him ways to foster the Canadian Pacific Railway's power in the city and in Ontario's southwestern region. In the fall of 1905 Carling arranged for him to make a series of visits to factories in Sarnia, Stratford, Waterloo, Brantford, and other nearby smaller cities. This was an unfamiliar world where Carling gave real help over the next year. In a follow-up meeting, the old businessman/politician suggested further ways for the

CPR to keep control of traffic in the goods produced in these and other places near London. Arthur deduced a general signal from these meetings: where the Grand Trunk emphasized links with the United States, the Canadian Pacific should strengthen the sense of an all-Ontario service. He continued to work assiduously over the next year to expand this aspect of his company's position in southwestern Ontario.

In his own office, he sensed trouble rising from a different alignment: not Canadian Pacific versus Grand Trunk, but management versus workers. London had a fairly stable labour force, so the Trainmen's Union was less militant here than it had been in Toronto. Yet as the months went by, there were often mutterings about low pay and long hours, a warning of trouble to come. Arthur strained to maintain peace while trying to wrestle the railway workers into compliance with his standards.

At the end of 1906, Arthur and Lizzie were called to a meeting that was destined to change their family life. In December, Bertha's school principal invited them in for an interview. She presented an excellent report on their daughter's academic work and attitude, and suggested that she should begin to prepare for university entrance exams, to be ready for college in the fall of '08. Arthur was startled. "But Bertha is a mere girl, Miss Murray."

"Girls aren't so mere any more, Mr. Smith."

On reflection, Arthur liked the idea of sending a daughter to university. He'd long ago given up the dream of having a son who might go to college, to become a lawyer maybe, or a doctor. Well now, why not prepare to offer higher education to his not-so-mere daughter? So Bertha spent the next year and a half adding an appropriate degree of serious study to her happy friendships at the Academy. She also developed subtle ways of snubbing her younger sister, which Zoë ignored in her own happy days at Talbot Public School.

For her part, Linzie concentrated on teaching Bertha how to make peach pie, and featherweight tea biscuits, and chocolate mousse, and five-layer lemon cake. This was appropriate training for a young lady turned sixteen, whether or not she became a college student in 1908. Lizzie herself continued to supply the basics at dinner time: chicken with dumplings, roast beef with Yorkshire pudding, chicken fricassees from the leftover chicken, beef hash from the roast, and then sausages and liver and onions to round out the week. Lizzie and Zoë, running on endless energy, were both slender, but Bertha grew more curvaceous every month, and Arthur became, in the euphemism of the day, a rather "portly" man. He was still tall but no longer thin. He now looked more like a manager.

Lizzie's life in London would remain in her memory forever as a halcyon time, a time of ease and good taste and congenial neighbours: everything a modern young matron could desire. Perhaps London, compared to Toronto, was a little provincial, a little insular, but it was easy to sink into total acceptance of London's opinion of itself as the pleasantest place in Canada.

Peace descended on the London house in the final months of family life there.

The halcyon time could not last. Arthur was destined to be moved once again. A special telegraph landed on his desk late on a Friday afternoon in the fall of 1907, advising that D.C. Coleman, on his way to the west coast, would drop in for a short visit. Mr. Coleman, who had risen through the ranks in Winnipeg, was rumoured to be slated to become head of the CPR's western lines. The two men had met several times at friendly Company gatherings. Mr. Coleman smiled as he came into Arthur's office saying "Good to see you, A.L."

Arthur smiled. "You too, D.C." Then the visitor announced without preamble that he had come to talk about a promotion—and another move. In July, 1908, "A.L." was to move to national headquarters in Montreal, as Train and Station Inspector for the Montreal district. That district was experiencing serious trouble with its labour force. The Trainmen's Union was making unreasonable demands, fomenting slowdowns, and threatening strikes. A.L. Smith, known for his effective relations with the labour force, would be reassigned to the Quebec district.

Arthur was of course flattered by the Company's confidence in him. Justified confidence, he felt, since he had always dealt effectively with the working people. He worried slightly about a job in Quebec since he did not speak French. But that was not his major concern. He had to say, "I must talk this over with my wife."

Mr. Coleman smiled. "I believe you will both enjoy the change. Although Montreal is not a pretty little place like London, it is a metropolis, and the headquarters of Canadian power."

Arthur had a momentary thought of dear Lizzie, still a pretty little person (to him, anyway) but also a power figure, and one that would pit her power against a move away from her well-loved London. "It sounds very interesting," he said. A handshake sealed an unspoken deal.

Arthur went home at the end of the day, proud to carry this affirmation of his employers' respect for him. But how would Lizzie react?

The answer was, tempestuously.

"A move to the central office is bound to be a good one," Arthur explained carefully.

Lizzie did not see things the same way. "I have had enough moves," she cried. Arthur kissed her and whispered comfort. Eventually Lizzie smiled again, tight-lipped.

Bertha and Zoë were far from tight-lipped when they were told that they would be leaving London in July. Zoë's woe was not dramatic. She simply sniffled at her desk in Talbot School until her teacher drifted down the aisle to ask what was troubling her. Zoë released a whimper of grief over a break in life, a change of home and playmates.

Bertha's louder woe quickly infected her schoolmates. Miss Murray, recognizing her inability to quell a classroom full of such grief, ended her history lesson abruptly and led her senior class for a walk around Victoria Park. She felt that the Smiths' leaving was unfortunate. Bertha, though a good student of history and literature, would have to work hard in science and mathematics to get into university. Not a good time to spend the winter in a disrupted home.

And what would Bertha do in the summer, after her school-leaving examinations, Lizzie wondered. Should she pack her belongings in July and take them to Montreal, only to pack again in September when she moved into college in Toronto in the fall? Arthur didn't know the answer.

Lizzie sat at the desk in the sunroom to write her weekly letter to Aurora. "Dearest Mother," she wrote. Then her hand froze and the pen dropped from unwilling fingers. Bertha took over the task. *"Dearest Grandma,"* she wrote, *"I hope you are feeling well. We have had some unsettling news. Father is being moved to Montreal. As you can imagine this is not easily accepted. Mother does not feel up to writing just now, so I am filling in! Zoë tries to help plan for the move, but of course she is too young to be much use! - With love from Bertha."*

ten

Siding
Transcontintal, 1907

Arthur cleared his desk in the CPR London office and prepared to move to Montreal in a mood of optimism. The move would be hard on the family, there was no doubt of that, but on the whole Arthur felt that since the family depended on him it must accept the dominance of his interests.

Zoë would transfer next fall from Ontario's five-year collegiate system to Quebec's four-year high school program. How would she cope with the summer months in Montreal? Would she be able to find friends before she enrolled in a new school in September?

Bertha would face different problems in the fall, as she returned to Toronto to enter university. But at least the question about her summer was settled. Grandma Baldwin's cousin Mearle Baldwin Gordon had written from Winnipeg recently, saying how much she would enjoy playing hostess this summer to one of the Baldwin grandchildren. Cousin Mearle was married to James T. Gordon, a successful entrepreneur, rancher, meat packer, and politician. Since their two sons were grown up and away, Mearle's distinguished husband agreed that it would be good to have a young person in their big house this summer.

Grandma first thought of suggesting her great-niece Eola Jaffray, who now lived in Sudbury, as the summer visitor. Then she wondered if Bertha should be the one to accept Mearle's invitation. Or maybe Bertha and Eola could travel together to Winnipeg and both enjoy Mearle's kind offer of hospitality.

"Who is Eola Jaffray?" Bertha asked when the plan was presented to her. Grandma wrote back, "Don't you remember? She lived in Aurora when you were here for your first year at school." Bertha didn't remember, but Arthur and Lizzie were delighted to accept anyway, as were Eola's parents.

Arthur arranged a railway pass to bring Eola from Sudbury to London at the end of June so that the girls could become reacquainted before leaving for the west. Once he would have scruples about using a Company pass for his family's pleasures; now he felt secure in his authority to bend rules, and he ordered railway passes for both girls on the Canadian Pacific transcontinental train. Just this year a direct line from Toronto to Sudbury made it possible to go west without first swerving east to Montreal.

Arthur suggested that he would also arrange passage for Bertha and Eola to go all the way to the west coast at the end of their Winnipeg stay. They could visit his brother Lincoln in Vancouver. This seemed to be a good time to revive connections with at least one of his family: Arthur's brothers had scattered over the continent, leaving the Major and Grandma Jane in Toronto with their daughter Natalie.

Cousin Mearle responded to this idea by promising to accompany the girls to Vancouver as a chaperone. Whereupon her husband Jim Gordon agreed to go with them as far as Calgary, where he had business to do with ranchers and meat packers.

Eola and her father arrived from Sudbury on the day after Bertha's last exam. After a brief supercilious circling around each other, the two  seventeen-year-old girls settled into warm friendship. Current photographs caught significant differences between them: Bertha, dark-haired, and pensive; Eola, blond,  and strong-minded. But they discovered a common sense of fun.

For Arthur, Bertha's western trip seemed unlike the short separations in the past when Lizzie or one of the girls left home for a brief visit to Aurora. It was as if he and Lizzie and Zoë were now being shunted onto a siding, while Bertha rode away to the west along the main track, coming back just in time to move into college residence. Or, perhaps more accurately, he and Lizzie and Zoë were on the main track, and Bertha's jaunt to the west and to university was itself just a shift onto a siding, a temporary separation from her family. At any rate, he would miss his pretty daughter.

On June the thirtieth, 1908, Bertha and Eola mounted the steps into the Pullman car of the westward bound train. They wore long dusters over their light-coloured dresses, the kind of dusters that motorists wore to protect their clothes from street dust. Nothing, however, could protect riders in the train cars. In this hot weather it was imperative that the windows be open, but open windows meant flying cinders and smut entering the cars and alighting on travellers. Brushing down the dusters simply made the dirt more likely to smear; the girls soon gave up any effort to stay clean.

They watched the gradual shift from southern Ontario farmland through the barren landscape in the northwest into the strange and awesome wilderness north of Lake Superior. At each station they descended from the train car, usually to find a station master alerted to their coming by a telegram from Bertha's anxious father, checking cheerfully to be sure the girls were enjoying the trip.

"Very much!" they told the succession of questioners. The truest part of that sturdy answer was the joy of sleeping in the Pullman car after the porter had made up the double bunk. Eola and Bertha took turns in the upper berth, so that each could savour the strange joy of peeping out of the nighttime window at the world they were passing through.

Finally, after Lake of the Woods and Kenora came the gentler land in Manitoba, and then they drew in at the busy Winnipeg station, with glimpses of the western city in the distance.

They arrived very hot and very dirty. "Welcome, my dears!" cried cousin Mearle, a tall lady, as excited as they were. "Call me Aunt Mearle, dears," she cried. "Uncle Jim," though not so elated, handed the two pretty young women into his notable automobile and then led them into his palatial house. His mansion made memories of Lady Carling's handsome London home seem insipid.

Yet the welcome was warm and exciting. "I know you are very tired, my dears," Mearle said, "But I couldn't wait to introduce my young friends to you!" She had organized an evening party. The girls barely had time for a cup of tea and a little nap before the house filled with the daughters of Mearle's friends, plus a number of young men newly come to the expanding city: young professionals and bankers and engineers, and a couple of accountants from Jim Gordon's business. All the young people clustered happily in the baronial-style reception room, grouping and regrouping.

One man, introduced as Dr. Craig McLaren, took a long look at Bertha's pretty, flushed young face and quietly asked, "May I show her your famous garden, Mrs. Gordon?"

"We'll all go outdoors, Craig!" Mearle cried. "You too, Eola! All of us!" and the whole party moved out to exclaim at the roses and peonies.

Something unpredictable had happened, however. The hard-working, ambitious young doctor had seen something in Bertha that moved him strangely. As the party ended, he asked Mearle for permission to take Bertha for a Sunday drive around the city. Mearle said, "If you include Eola and me, yes." Then she asked, just above a whisper, "Do you realize how young Bertha is?" and answered her own question, "She's just seventeen."

"I see." The young doctor saw his own studious self at seventeen, grimly concentrating on pre-med and medical studies, forgoing any romantic impulses. He confessed to Mearle that his reaction to Bertha was something new to him—and something meaningful. Mearle Gordon, sympathetic but perplexed by this assault on her first day as a chaperone, ended the conversation by accepting the offer of a Sunday tour in his motor car.

It was the first of many outings. Mearle was taken along on innumerable rides, listening to Craig explain about his practice and his prospects. He had few chances to speak directly to Bertha about his sudden hope that she would someday become part of his life. Wild roses bloomed in profusion on the sideroads outside Winnipeg: "Pretty, like you!" Craig said.

By the time the visit in Winnipeg was over, Bertha was in a state of confusion. Neither Parkdale nor London had given her any experience in adolescent flirtations. Now suddenly here was a determined adult suitor, intent on telling her every day about his delight in her company. Bertha was glad that Aunt Mearle was usually hovering.

Eola, as another newcomer to Winnipeg society, acquired her own circle of admirers, but nothing like this. How much should they tell their parents in letters home? Keeping a secret proved to be more fun than coping with the young man's visits.

To Bertha's relief, Mearle organized the day of departure from Winnipeg for the trip to Vancouver so that there was no time for visits from Dr. McLaren or anyone else. Mearle had checked and expanded the girls' wardrobes for their foray with her into the far west of the Dominion. Uncle Jim would go with them as far as Calgary. He was left to pack his own valise.

Winnipeg was forgotten as the prairies rushed past the train windows, giving way to the foothills, and finally to the marvellous vision of the Rocky Mountains. The girls swung down at every stop in the journey, never too tired to see new sights and to write them up in their daily journals. Mearle smiled, read her book, and admitted to herself that she found young girls very exhausting. Nevertheless, once in Vancouver

she took them to see the deep ravine called "the flume." How terrifying to walk across the ravine on a swaying wooden bridge—almost too exciting to be photographed!

In Vancouver they also visited Bertha's Uncle Lincoln. He was full of jokes—unlike his serious brother Arthur. He gave Bertha a memorial silver spoon to take to her father, engraved "Prince Rupert, 1908." He told

Bertha that it celebrated the Grand Trunk Railway's conclusion of a second transcontinental railway. "Your father will appreciate this," he laughed. Bertha wasn't sure that a token of Grand Trunk achievement would be so very welcome.

Then back Bertha and Eola travelled to Winnipeg for another few weeks. Dropping in at tea time on the final day of the visit, Dr. McLaren at last seized a chance to read a "little poem" he had composed in Bertha's honour:

> *Red roses are pretty, and so are the pink,*
> *But the prettiest rose, I really do think*
> *Is wild-rose Miss Bertha, so dainty and sweet*
> *From the top of her head to her two tiny feet.*

Bertha hastily tucked her not-so-tiny feet under her skirts, while Eola developed a coughing fit that drove her from the room. "I tell you what, Bertha," she said later, "He's not Heathcliff. Not even Mr. Rochester. And all this stuff about roses is just moonshine." Bertha had no ready answer.

Next morning a crowd of Aunt Mearle's young friends came to the station, many bearing gifts. Craig McLaren thrust a handsomely wrapped book into Bertha's hands. He was smiling brightly, but his final handshake lingered. Uncle Jim helped the girls board the homeward train. Cousin Mearle waved to her two pretty guests with a certain amount of relief.

In Toronto, Eola's father had come from Sudbury to meet her and take her home. Bertha stayed on the eastbound train until it reached Montreal the next morning. Arthur, Lizzie, and Zoë met her at the Windsor Station and whisked her by taxi to their new home in Westmount.

Lizzie and Zoë had arrived in Montreal only a few days earlier. "What about me?" Zoë had asked in the wake of Bertha's trip west. "When do I go on a fancy tour?" Clearly it was politic to devise a summer trip for the younger, irritated, jealous sister. Lizzie found a Canadian Pacific Railway brochure and proposed that she and Zoë would enjoy a jaunt on their own. Arthur agreed. Another small separation from the family—but his first summer on the job in Montreal would allow hardly any time for family life anyway. "Fair's fair," he said. "And you deserve a little side trip too."

Lizzie and Zoë had barely touched down in their new home in Montreal before leaving for a tour to the east. They travelled to Quebec City by train, boarded a steamboat there, and sailed down the St. Lawrence River to Tadoussac for a memorable time in the CPR hotel there. So Zoë

felt no resentment regarding Bertha's trip out west, but cheerfully concentrated at the end of August on getting ready for her entrance into Westmount High School.

Arthur had found an acceptable house on Sherbrooke Street in Westmount. He lived in it alone for July and August. He was too preoccupied with his new duties to feel very lonely. In his office in the Windsor Station downtown he felt that he was part of modern Montreal, the centre of power in the Canadian railway world, as in all the other Canadian worlds of significance in this first decade of the twentieth century. All the major concerns—insurance companies, banks, manufacturing businesses, department stores—were headquartered in Montreal, still Canada's major city. He was certainly not on a siding now.

eleven

Strikes
Montreal, 1908

Over the summer Arthur gave himself a quick course in local operations, not by physically visiting all the nearby stations, but by studying the charts and memos and reports in the head office in Montreal. He also introduced himself to his opposite numbers in other areas of railway management: the accountant, the construction engineers, the lawyers, the senior staff in the food and supply commissaries. Then he returned to his earlier preoccupation: stepping out of the office to visit the actual operations.

First, he went down to the working level beneath the office floors in Windsor Station. Here the multiple rails connected and diverged, and the myriad trains, local and continental, arrived and departed. And here, from the time he began work as Inspector of Trains and Stations in Montreal in July, 1908, he heard talk of labour unrest.

Since his days as telegrapher, he had worked with engineers, conductors, firemen, and brakemen, most of them organized as members in one of the Running Trades Brotherhoods, such as the Order of Railway Conductors. The Canadian Pacific was a pioneer in negotiating with such unions. But this year, in an economic downturn, many of the trainmen had suffered a pay cut, or had been demoted to a more junior rank, and the Brothers were ready to express anger to a new representative of the Company management.

Arthur had always been on good terms not only with many of the employees on the trains but also with the builders and repairers of tracks. Now, as he ventured beyond the station to the Windsor yards, he sensed trouble in their ranks also. They knew that construction of competing transcontinental lines was nearing completion now out west, causing wide-scale layoffs of outside workers in the prairie provinces. Dread of similar unemployment infected workmen in the Windsor yards.

Arthur's uneasiness grew as he moved beyond the centre of Montreal to nearby smaller stations in Westmount, Montreal Junction, Laval, and Bordeaux. Here he met a third group of workers, station agents, telegraphers, and baggage handlers. For these people, the Company had always provided housing, like Arthur's first house in Aurora, and since 1903 it had also guaranteed their pensions on retirement. Now the agents spoke to him of their dread that these advantages might be withdrawn as the economy faltered.

A fourth world of "railway people," new to him, appeared when he visited the sprawling Angus Shops. These great factory-like workplaces had opened in 1904 down in the Glen, closer to the river than Windsor Station. Here craftsmen created and assembled new rolling stock and re-tooled old engines and cars. Arthur met machinists, blacksmiths, carpenters, and boilermakers, each man belonging to his own craft union. They told him that the CPR had signed agreements with them and they hoped a strike could be avoided. But, they muttered, since July there had been unacceptable hiring of ill-equipped and underpaid apprentices. They believed these attacks on their self-respect reflected an anti-union attitude drifting up from the United States. The shop's craft workers admitted that they were ready to strike.

Canadian laws affirmed the need of arbitration, but this time the Labour Arbitration Board's pro-worker conclusions were rejected by both the Canadian Pacific and the Grand Trunk (which was reportedly more anti-union than the CPR). In 1907 the new Industrial Disputes Investigation Act had introduced ways to reduce labour strikes, and on this basis the CPR declared its willingness to make concessions in July of 1908. But after a year of unrest, job cuts, and reclassifications, workers prepared to take action.

On August 5, 1908, when Arthur had barely settled into his new position, outside workers in the Canadian west, both at the Grand Trunk and the Canadian Pacific, went on strike. Labourers in the sorting yards behind the Windsor Station threatened similar action in Montreal. A general strike that might cripple both giant companies was declared on August 8.

Arthur badly needed relief and distraction from all these difficulties. When his women-folk returned from their travels at the end of summer he gladly forgot about the ongoing strike for the moment and settled into soothing domestic patterns. He was almost pathetically happy to help Bertha plan her college courses, listen to Zoë fussing about her new high school middy-and-skirt uniform, and ratify Lizzie's new dependence on a Chinese laundry to cope with the increasing burden of washing, bleaching, and ironing his shirts and starched collars, as well as the girls' blouses and petticoats and the household linen. Lizzie recalled with a shudder the alternative endured when the girls were small: the heavy tubs, the washboard, the irons that had to be heated on the wood stove. "Thank goodness we live in the modern age, my dear," Arthur said and avoided telling her about his modern-age troubles.

He took Lizzie and the girls in a calèche up the Montreal mountain, to the lookout where fashionable Montrealers joined the tourists in admiring the panorama spread out before them. "Look— we can see all the way to the United States!"

Next day Lizzie and Bertha took a cab along Sherbrooke Street into downtown Montreal to visit Holt Renfrew's store, which carried the newest styles from New York. "We will just look at the fashions, Bertha," Lizzie said, "then we will find a good dressmaker to copy the details for us." Good intentions; but the array of charming dresses, floating in an atmosphere of eau de cologne and ferried back and forth by a bevy of stylish salesladies, undid Lizzie's resolve. She and Bertha each arrived home with an outfit, "straight from New York" and devastatingly expensive.

Home life in Westmount offered a strange contrast to the work world at Windsor Station. The strike was definitely on. The CPR announced that it would hire men "to fill the vacancies caused by the strike." Early in September, the company advertised heavily in British papers for first-class workers: "Only competent and reliable men need apply." There were some signs of sabotage at the Montreal railway terminal and also at the Angus Yards, and ragged attacks on the strikebreakers.

Non-Canadian workers replaced the strikers in many jobs under Arthur's jurisdiction. British workers, both English and Scottish, arrived by ship in Montreal and went to work. Some of the accents reminded Arthur of his father's lingering mannerisms. He gravely watched the imported labourers at work in the Windsor yards, stumbling through work in unfamiliar settings.

At home, he found Bertha packing a big suitcase as she prepared to enter her own new world at St. Hilda's, the women's residence for Trinity College in Toronto. Near the bottom she slipped in *Golden Gleams of Thought*, given her by Craig McLaren when she left Winnipeg. On top of it, she placed her real choice of reading: *Pride and Prejudice*, *Wuthering Heights*, and this year's bestseller, *Anne of Green Gables*. Next came the black academic gown, as specified by the College, which required that it be worn to every lecture. Finally, she packed her New York dress.

Zoë was offered last year's dress. "Hand-me-downs!" she cried. Everyone in her new high school would notice! Bertha closed the lid of her trunk and went to take her place at the dinner table for the last time. Her father could only hope she would find that life at college offered more joy than he was finding at work.

Arthur had received a carefully worded letter from a Dr. McLaren in Winnipeg, who mentioned his background—Dalhousie Medical

School and a growing practice—and then asked permission to correspond with Bertha while she was at college. He ended by referring to Bertha's wild-rose beauty. Arthur looked up from his dish of lamb stew. The young doctor was right: Bertha's dark hair, sparkling grey eyes, and gently rounded figure combined into a graceful, pretty sight (though Arthur thought that Lizzie, with her blue eyes and slim form, was still prettier). The young doctor's devotion seemed understandable. But Arthur must not be distracted, he told himself, as the lemon meringue pie appeared. He would answer the young doctor's letter, permitting the correspondence. College would probably so absorb Bertha that a distant suitor would soon be forgotten.

As it turned out, college life wasn't all fun. Bertha's first formal class at Trinity College was traumatic. Women had been inching into university classes for twenty years now, but in tiny numbers and mostly in the form of bespectacled bookworms easily ignored by the lords of academe. Bertha was part of the drift of a new kind of "co-ed": ready to be studious, yes, but far from a blue-stockinged intellectual. Yet she heard whispered taunts and sneers during fifty uncomfortable minutes of her first English class, while the professor blithely ignored the male rumblings; ignored, also, the young woman who was the object of the whispering campaign.

When the class ended, Bertha scurried away as fast as her hobble skirt would let her run. Three apologetic young men hustled after her. "Sorry!" "We didn't mean to offend you!" "We're glad to have ladies in our class!" But they weren't really glad, Bertha suspected.

Soon, however, their rejection was forgotten. She proudly sent home a photograph of the "Freshettes" lined up as "Class of 1912" in their academic gowns, each with a tidy bun at the back of her head. Bertha, as shortest girl in her class, was last in the lineup. A few days later she tried out for the college choir. The choirmaster said she had the makings of a really fine voice—and made an appointment for her to enroll in a vocal-training program at the Royal Conservatory of Music.

Back in Montreal, Zoë had become involved in in a different kind of interest: national politics. A federal election was scheduled for October. The grade nine history teacher at Westmount High undertook to inculcate her own Liberal support for Wilfrid Laurier into her students. Zoë's new friend Dora Braidwood confessed that her family were Conservative but that she would vote for Laurier if she had a chance. "We'll have a chance someday," Zoë said. "I'm a suffragette," she confided. "But don't tell my family."

Arthur was not pleased by Zoë's love of Laurier. This Prime Minister had foolishly listened to the argument presented to him in 1896 by C.M. Hays, the general manager of the Grand Trunk Railway, that Canada needed a second transcontinental railway. That decision had now created disastrous financial problems, making the government less than friendly to all railways. Arthur was feeling the pinch of government austerity in his own work.

Mercifully, late in October after some ugly incidents the strike ended. The CPR managers dismissed the no-longer-needed strikebreakers and welcomed the return of regular workers. Disgruntled British men trudged across the Montreal docks onto the boats that would carry this "competent and reliable" group home. How could Arthur help the Company shift back from alien strikebreakers to the reinstated Canadian employees? Many of the "regular employees" were French speakers, which made it hard for Arthur to talk to them. Yet he had to soothe the hostile feelings that remained after the strike ended, whether expressed in French or English.

A man sitting across from Arthur at lunch in the Company dining room advised him to get in touch with the French-Canadian agent at Viger Station. "He probably has a plan for after the strike." Arthur left the lunch room and started toward Viger Station on foot. Situated in the French-speaking centre of Montreal, Viger rivalled Windsor Station in significance and outshone it in charm.

This visit involved Arthur in an unexpected bilingual experience. He introduced himself to the station agent, Matthieu Fichaud, and was drawn at once into a proposal. Would Arthur talk to the English speakers among the Viger personnel? A little word about the end of the strike and the good times to begin again? In return, M. Fichaud promised to come to Windsor and give a talk to the francophones there, now that the strike had ended. Arthur agreed with pleasure. Then M. Fichaud led him out behind the impressive façade to the yard where multiple tracks lay beneath snow-proof roofing. Arthur had fallen into an unusual  connection. Theoretically, he was inspector of all trains and operations in Montreal; but rarely did a man in his position find as friendly an entrée into the French part of the city.

Hardly had the strike been settled before the returning workers began to raise further claims. Men in the terminal threatened to strike again unless their wages were raised to equal those of their counterparts working in major railways in the United States. Arthur pleaded their cause with higher-ups in the Canadian Pacific and tried to pacify the disgruntled workers. But even after the acceptance of a compromise with the Brotherhoods, the men announced once more their readiness to strike. Montreal buzzed with news that after the autumn strike ended, the Company had broken its promise to rehire 250 of the strikers. Those workers who were rehired found that their pensions had been discontinued. Worse still, they had been stripped of the privilege of living in their Company-owned houses.

A sad business, and for Arthur it coincided with a more personal blow for his family. A shattering letter came from Aurora. Grandma Baldwin, never really herself since Anah's death, had suffered a stroke. Within a week a second stroke proved fatal. Lizzie took Zoë to Aurora for the funeral, hoping that her youthful spirit would help Grandpa endure the period of mourning. They would leave Arthur on his own for a while in Montreal. "Can you manage?"

Arthur privately thought that a week without female chatter might be a welcome break. Aloud he admitted that though he would be lonely he could, with difficulty, manage. He would stay alone in the Westmount house that the Company had found for him.

There the reunited family spent a subdued Christmas. Bertha, home for the holidays, tried to give a Quebec touch to Christmas by creating a "Bûche de Noël" in place of the traditional plum pudding. There was no talk about strikes in the quiet house, but not much joy either.

twelve

Wrecks

Farnham, 1909-10

After Christmas, Lizzie proudly showed the official photo of Bertha in academic garb to her new Westmount friends, Mrs. Macarthur and Mrs. Struthers. Each was a sister-in-law of earlier friends, one in London and one in Parkdale. Neighbouring ladies also came to the house to pay formal calls. Zoë, not entirely graciously, agreed to pass the cups of tea and the dishes of poppyseed cake.

Arthur Lloyd Smith enjoyed few such pleasant times at work in Montreal. On one cold day in March, he witnessed a terrible accident. A spring suddenly broke in the engine of a train from Boston running toward Windsor Station. The boiler, breached, sent deadly jets of scalding steam into the cab. The fireman jumped; the engineer stayed until he was thrown from the cab and died. The driverless train careened into the station. Although a gateman ran along the platform, shouting and pushing people out of danger, four bystanders waiting to greet passengers were killed. The train then crashed through the stone wall into the passenger concourse and on into the ladies' waiting room, killing a woman and three children there. While the engine sank through the floor and passenger cars collapsed, the baggage car smashed on through the outside wall, and ended up hanging over a short street near Bonsecours market. Like the 1895 crash at the Montparnasse station in Paris, this Montreal accident was widely covered in the international press.

Arthur was in his office upstairs at the time, but he shared the public shock and horror of the crash. His old personal terror of accidents intensified. Early in his career, a CPR train going north from London toward Sarnia had ended in a terrible train wreck that caught comparable

international attention. The *New York Times* carried a story back then, suggesting that a telegraph operator's error had caused the wreck and the death of more than a score of people. This had remained a nightmare for Arthur, who still identified with all telegraphers.

Now, as Train and Station Inspector for Montreal, he had to sit through the harrowing follow-up meetings and official discussions of the Windsor station wreck. His old personal terror of accidents intensified.

Later in the spring of 1909, he suffered a minor but more personal shock. For some time, Bertha had been writing home about the increasing difficulty of her university courses. At her final examinations, she suffered badly from nerves. Her final college marks in May showed that she was right to be nervous. Her results were dismal: no "A's," one "B" in English Literature, "C's" in English, History, and Geometry, and she had failed two courses, French and Biology. Arthur took time off work to go to Toronto and speak to the Dean of Arts. He was met with sympathy and an explanation that many young women were not properly prepared for the rigours of university. Miss Murray's academy had not provided a solid foundation, and Bertha had not worked hard enough to compensate. This offered little comfort to Arthur, but at least he learned that his daughter could write supplementals in August. If she proved successful then, she could return to college in the fall.

Failure was less of a blow to Bertha than to her father. She took comfort in having won high praise at the Toronto Conservatory of Music and in having enjoyed a happy year and made very good friends. At the Varsity skating rink, she had met a young engineering student named Jim Laing. He told her he came from Sudbury, and was a good friend of Eola Jaffray's there. As the college year went by, Jim exploited his connection with Eola and became Bertha's steady partner at tea dances in St. Hilda's.

Soon after the disastrous end of her first year in college, Bertha was pleased to be invited to spend a month in Sudbury with Eola. The northern mining town was rather chaotic, but being with Eola was a joy, and so was Jim Laing's tendency to drop by the Jaffrays' house on the way home from his summer job at the steel company.

Arthur underwent a less pleasant change as the summer of 1909 came to an end. The CPR management directed him to do a stint of work in Farnham. This small city, situated below the St. Lawrence River, about forty miles southeast of Montreal, was a hub of connections to northeastern American states: Maine, Vermont, and upstate New York. He was needed there because of timetabling problems caused by the growth of traffic between Montreal and the American border. It would be a brief assignment, probably lasting less than a year, and it would bring a promotion with it. He would move back to his office in Windsor Station not as Inspector of Trains and Stations in Montreal but as Chief Inspector of Trains and Stations in the Montreal Region.

Arthur had a puzzled feeling that he was being shunted away from the centre of power in Montreal. Perhaps his sympathy for the striking workers had not been as secret as he had hoped? Or maybe his friendship with francophone M. Fichaud, the manager at Viger station, was not welcomed by the very anglophone managers at Windsor Station?

As he considered the map that centred in Farnham, he reached a more soothing conclusion. Canadian Pacific connections with American railways were clearly marked at the busy Farnham junction. The Central Vermont, the Montreal Portland and Boston, and the Delaware and Hudson Railway lines all met in Farnham. Arthur could see the need to keep all these lines running south from Montreal effectively interlocked and active.

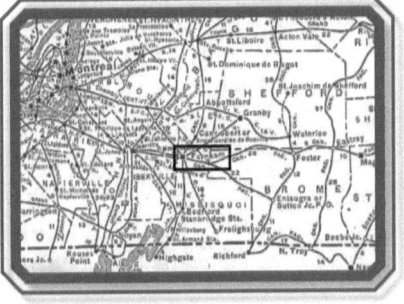

His map also showed an alternative route to the United States. The Grand Trunk Railway ran from Montreal to Rouse's Point in upstate New York, on a line through St. Johns, just west of Farnham. In his work here, as in his earlier work in London, Arthur was probably expected to further CPR interests and to thwart those of the Grand Trunk, in the ongoing rivalry for American connections.

Whatever its political value, a move to Farnham sounded to Lizzie like a disaster. Zoë would have to move to an unknown school in Farnham, just when she was settling so well into Westmount High School. Would she wind up like Bertha, underprepared for a future shift to university? And how would Bertha weather another move before returning to college in September? Lizzie did not mention her personal dismay at the prospect of yet another house in another town, without hope of another friend like Mrs. Macarthur or Mrs. Struthers turning up.

Arthur decided that he would move alone to Farnham. He could occupy the furnished apartment near the Farnham station that the Company promised to provide, and come back to Montreal on weekends. He thought sadly of the way the tracks divided beyond Farnham. It seemed to portray the way his family was separating, following different lines.

As he settled into a new life as an absentee father, living in Farnham apart from Lizzie and Zoë, he found some comfort in news from Bertha. With successful "supps" behind her, she celebrated her nineteenth birthday in late September and was installed again at Toronto for her second college year, 1909–10. Her classmates rechristened her "Buffy." ("Since Bertha is rather an old-fashioned name, if you don't mind us mentioning it!") Her music teachers announced that her voice was developing beautifully under Royal Conservatory direction. Life unfolded quietly and happily: lots of lectures, lots of essays. And, increasingly, lots of skating and dancing parties, lots of nice young men at the parties, usually now including Jim Laing. Her correspondence with Dr. Craig McLaren continued in the winter of 1910. But her study habits languished. She was on the way to a second failed year.

Arthur, unaware of his older daughter's imminent troubles, concentrated on Zoë. In early spring, after his weekend visit home, he

took her with him to Farnham and introduced her to his colleagues there. They travelled farther, toward the American border. A photographer took a picture of them with the Lake Megantic station master and an assorted group of railway workers and bystanders. Zoë wore a plain ankle-length dress appropriate for a fifteen-year-old. Arthur wore his executive wing collar and tie but struck a casual pose designed to put the Company's employees at ease.

He was no longer the slender man he had been when he married Lizzie. The Farnham hotel, a famous regional dining facility, offered roast beef and Yorkshire pudding, with browned potatoes and onions and rich dark gravy. That suited Arthur all too well. By the end of his time in Farnham he had added two gold links to his watch chain. It looped more tautly now from the fob in the pocket on the left of his waistcoat to the gold watch in the pocket on the right. The gold watch itself was nicely engraved to mark it as a parting gift from his admiring Toronto associates.

His soft brown hair had gradually receded, leaving a calm high forehead destined to reassure fellow-workers of his quiet common sense.

Lizzie and his daughters still considered him the handsomest man in Canada.

The CPR in Montreal also appreciated him, if less adoringly, and welcomed him back to the office in Windsor Station for another stint. One day in the fall of 1910 he joined a group of his colleagues for lunch at a club on Beaver Hall Hill. In a sudden hush, all eyes turned to watch a commanding figure come in. A whisper ran, "That's Charles Melville Hays." Arthur watched the progress across the room of the famous—or, to CPR personnel, infamous—head of the Grand Trunk Railway. Arthur thought with a smile

 that long ago this man had been the head of the company he worked for in Aurora. To his surprise, Mr. Hays paused and caught Arthur's eye. "A.L. Smith, isn't it?" he said. "I keep hearing about you. Someday you'll hear from me and maybe I'll steal you back!" He laughed. Before Arthur could think of a reply, the great man was gone. Arthur was left to explain to his colleagues that he had indeed been a GTR man, "Long ago, when I didn't know any better!"

The fall of 1910 held no such happy moments for Bertha. A second year of low marks had eliminated her chances of returning easily to university next year. She decided to forgo the chance to write supplemental exams, and withdrew from Trinity College. It was hard to read a letter from her former roommate Bea Wallace, bubbling with anticipation of third-year activities. Another letter arrived from Jim Laing: "So it's true you are leaving the University of Toronto? That does seem too bad!"

Yes, it really was too bad—and nobody seemed to care. Dr. McLaren, her erstwhile suitor, also wrote to her still, but at longer intervals, discouraged no doubt by her own infrequent correspondence. A cool autumnal letter from him ended,

"I am thinking of you tonight, Bertha, and sorry to hear that you have had an unhappy time lately. I myself have had a holiday, a fishing trip that I shall always remember.

As ever, Craig."

Bertha found an apt quotation in the *Golden Gleams* book: *"We bury Love; Forgetfulness grows over it, like grass."*

Some consolation came with another letter from Jim Laing, announcing his plan to come to Montreal for the big Toronto-McGill football game in October. "Your friend Bea Wallace will come along if she can stay at your house."

The 1910 football weekend turned out very well. Bea and Bertha went with Jim to the McGill campus, where they posed on a park bench for a picture: Bertha with a big bow on her hat, Bea with a posy in her hand; both beaming, despite any regrets.

Zoë's high school class also went to the big football game. Her gym teacher felt it would be good for students to see that side of college life in advance. Arthur felt he should mention that other aspects of college life were more important than football. "Yes, Father, yes, yes!" Zoë agreed. Arthur sharpened his glance. His younger daughter was a puzzle to  him. She did not behave like either Lizzie or Bertha. Did not look like them for that matter. More like his own side of the family, he admitted; her sharp features reminded him of his own mother.

Zoë's tumultuous progress had become the main feature of Lizzie's weekly letters to Aurora, addressed sadly now not to "Dearest Mother" but to "My dear Father."

In response, Grandpa Baldwin invited Zoë for a weekend visit to Aurora. He showed her the paintings by her still-celebrated Great-Aunt Anah. "Maybe you are something of an artist too, Zoë?"

"Not me, Grandpa," Zoë admitted. "Bertha is, though."

Grandpa moved on toward the back of the house. "Maybe you are the musician in the family? Your mother once wrote about your piano playing."

"Well, yes, but that was when I was young."

"What is your special interest, then, Zoë?"

"Politics, Grandpa."

"Good gracious!" He opened the back door and looked out at the autumnal garden.

Back home in Montreal, Zoë's obsession with politics now dominated the Smiths'

family life. The women teachers at her high school were leading a protest against their unequal pay. Zoë's classmates, male and female both, were agitated by sympathy. Zoë subjected her less radical family to dinnertime harangues about injustice, materialism, and old-fashioned conservatism.

Bertha, absorbed in neither fashion nor politics but in music, registered at the McGill Conservatory in the vocal performance classes. Madame Irina Koestler, a distinguished member there, accepted her as a student after Christmas. Madame was preparing Bertha for a performance, with the other students, in a summer recital at the Montreal Ladies' Morning Musicale. Breathing deeply from her diaphragm, she launched into her solo recital piece: "*Je suis Titania . . . la reine de l'aire.*" The lyric notes rose high and lovely. "*Sehr gut,*" said Madame (not known for giving praise).

Later, at the dinner table, Bertha was eager to tell her family about Madame Koestler's praise, but Zoë dashed in, waving ink-stained hands. Arthur bowed his head to say grace. "For what we are about to receive, may the Lord make us truly thankful. And make us mindful of the needs of others." Oblivious of the needs of others, Zoë swung into chatter about the toughness of Quebec matriculation examinations. Lizzie's suggestion of a little tea party this weekend was quashed with cries of horror and indignation. "You want me to fail my matric?"

Everyone looked forward to summer, when Lizzie could entertain her lady friends, Bertha would concentrate on Titania, and Zoë might survive her obsession with politics.

thirteen

Tracks
Lake Superior, 1911

Summer came, but traumatic change came too. The Company offered another promotion to A.L. Smith. As Chief Inspector of Trains and Stations in the Montreal Region, he held a position one notch beneath that of Superintendent. Now he was to move upward—and away from Montreal. A.L. Smith was to become Superintendent of the Lake Superior Division and to move to Sudbury as of July 1, 1911. A.L. Smith assured the CPR management that he was pleased with the prospective move.

"At least they waited long enough for Zoë to finish high school," said Lizzie. She had exhausted the ability to protest.

Bertha bewailed the lost chance of performing as Titania, but secretly thought that Sudbury would be nice. Eola was there, and Jim Laing also.

Zoë raised a howl of indignation. Then she realized that when fall came and the family lived in Sudbury, she would have to move into residence at McGill instead of living at home. An advantageous change? Her protests subsided.

Arthur travelled in advance of the family, to check the houses that the company offered for his inspection. His first glimpse of the countryside surrounding Sudbury was daunting, to say the least. When the  train left the pleasant hilly country west of Ottawa, it rattled through an empty world, sometimes forested, sometimes treeless. The railway cut through walls of rock, darkened by some black substance that seemed to stain the granite like grim lichen. To the north, barrens stretched, sparsely populated except for small Indian reservations and ghost towns marking unsuccessful mining operations.

An unpleasant smell permeated the train car: something sulfuric? Sulfur dioxide, emitted from the smelting plants? Then, as the train slowed when it approached Sudbury and crossed a spur junction, he forgot the odd odour. His eye was caught by strange hills of slag, heaped near the rough rails of the spur. A light rain was falling, but it could not disguise the stark ugliness of these heaps and hollows.

Arthur pulled his suitcase from the luggage stowed at the end of the car. The modest station that faced him as he descended was a far cry from the Windsor Station he had left behind in Montreal. He knew that this was one of the points of conflict between the town of Sudbury and the Canadian Pacific Railway: the failure to begin construction of a much needed, much larger station. The CPR alternate track from Montreal to Sudbury via Toronto had been declared complete in 1908, but the company had not seen fit to build a larger station then.

To his surprise, a tall young man greeted him as he stepped down from the railway car. "Mr. Smith! Welcome to Sudbury!" The young man proffered a deferential hand. "I'm McNair, Mickey McNair, the temporary station agent, sir." He snatched the bag from Arthur's hand and explained, "I have a gig here ready to take you to see some houses that might suit you."

Arthur tried to hide his confusion. He had not expected anyone to meet him. The young man pulled up a small stool to make it easier to hop up into the waiting carriage. Off they drove to look at houses that might suit the family. The first two were too far from the station to suit Arthur. But a large and rather impressive house stood at the corner of Elgin and Shaughnessy. There was no possible way Arthur could turn this house down. "Very nice indeed," he said, as he was shown the amenities of the big brick house. A small worry niggled at him: would this place seem pretentious to the people he would be directing and working with? Never mind, it was indeed very nice, and just the ticket for mollifying Lizzie.

Mickey McNair offered to settle him in for the night at the King Edward hotel, just across from the station. But Arthur wanted to take the night train back to Montreal.

Two days later, John, Mary, and Eola Jaffray were waiting at the Sudbury station to welcome Arthur, Lizzie, and their daughters. Lizzie hadn't seen her cousins since Grandma Baldwin's funeral, so there was a little sadness in the air, but the Jaffrays quickly whisked them off to their hospitable house. Here they would stay until the goods and chattels arrived from Montreal. Mary whispered, "I feel we're almost like sisters instead of just cousins by marriage." Lizzie harboured a dissenting opinion. "Just live with Bertha and Zoë for a couple of weeks and you'd know that sisterhood is not all that great!"

At the end of his first week, Arthur knew he needed a work space elsewhere than in the present station. The tiny office served Mickey McNair as telegrapher and station agent; and the passenger waiting room was also the baggage room, full of baggage.

While Zoë and Lizzie began setting their new home to rights, Arthur took Bertha to make the rounds of the butcher, the grocer, the baker, and the egg lady, introducing himself, and leaving orders to be delivered to the house. At the counter of the butcher shop a man who had piled up a big order of meat called out, "Hello, A.L.!"

"Hello, Dan!" Arthur answered happily, and quickly asked Bertha if she remembered the railway man who used to visit them in White River. Then he ignored her and dropped into a chat with his friend about progress on a bridge under construction to the west of Sudbury. After they left the store Bertha exclaimed, "My goodness, that man was buying an awfully big order of food!"

Her father laughed. "Well, he has five boys to feed."

They had barely arrived home when the same man knocked on the door. Bertha, answering the knock, was astonished when he said, "Before I say hello again to your father, I want to ask you, Miss Bertha, if you would like to go to a concert in the Town Hall this evening with me."

Her answer was barely polite, and she shut the door without inviting him in. "Imagine!" she huffed as she went back into the living room. "A father of five thinking I would go out with him!"

Her father smiled. "You've got it wrong, Bertha. My old friend Dan's a construction engineer in charge of a work gang of five men. Not a family man, I think." Seeing her embarrassment, he reassured her. "Never mind—you won't see him again. He's just here for a few days getting supplies before going back to the construction camp. I'll apologize for you when I run into him there."

A funny story to tell Eola, Bertha thought. Eola was obviously primed to tell her all about Jack Hammell, the Sudbury man she had been writing about all spring. But next day Bertha had someone else to talk about: Jim Laing came to call. He brought a letter from his mother, inviting Bertha for a week at their cottage on McGregor Bay. "My mother wants to meet you, because I've told her what a splendid skater you are and she was keen on skating when she was young. You can bring young Zoë along. I have two young sisters she will get along with." Jim would take a week's leave from his summer job to go to the cottage. "It's a great place, Buffy! Really wild!"

Further afield, Arthur would have to push for quicker construction of new track west of Sudbury. Since 1906, two transcontinental trains a week had been scheduled to steam in each direction along the tracks leading from Sudbury to Vancouver. In 1907 that number had grown to three a week during July and August. That was the schedule: the actual operation was often more ragged. By 1909, the company had completed a double set of tracks between Winnipeg and Fort William to cope with the ever-increasing loads of wheat moving from the prairies to the Lake Superior ships that would carry Canadian grain on the way to eastern Canada, and beyond, to Great Britain and Europe. But the stretch of rail on the north side of Lake Superior between For William and Sudbury—

the stretch that defined most of Arthur Smith's territory—remained single-tracked, except at a few minor junctions such as White River, and of course at Sudbury. Elsewhere along the line, the express trains had priority, and local trains had to be instructed to take the nearest siding, sometimes for a long and irritating time. This caused problems of communication and response. Sometimes the transcontinental express was held up by local trains that had not received or obeyed the right messages. It was imperative that Superintendent Smith choke off the jokes that were going around about the CPR's "non-express." Extra work gangs must eradicate those problem spots. The CPR's transcontinental trains had to snake north of the greatest of the Great Lakes without hindrance, and without infuriating the regular customers at each point along the route.

Closer to home, Sudbury people were calling insistently for a bigger and better CPR station. Agent Mickey McNair introduced the city dignitaries as they began to drop in to meet the new Superintendent. Frank McLeod, the newly elected mayor, Frank Cochrane, former mayor and now member of Parliament for the Nipissing district, and William McVittie and other long-time leaders in Sudbury all smilingly reminded him that an appropriate, handsome CPR station had been promised to Sudbury years ago. Though Arthur enjoyed meeting them all, he was only half-confident that he could manage to achieve their goal. But he said he would do his best.

Meanwhile, judging the smooth running of the transcontinental to be his major concern in his first summer on the job, he sallied forth, as Superintendent of the Lake Superior Division, into the western hinterlands. "A.L. Smith" quickly became an unmistakable part of the landscape in the area, walking around construction sites, clad in his long black coat, dark suit, and formal homburg hat. He made unexpected visits to work gangs along the line and became known for listening to the men's worries and com-

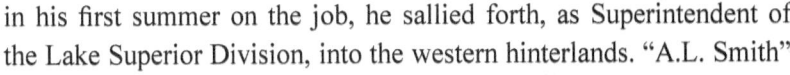

plaints and finding ways to solve labour problems.

The work force was very mixed. So many immigrant labourers were at odds with born-in-Canada veterans eager to protect their seniority. Other special problems rose in the outlying areas with the indigenous workers, who were motivated by a very different set of conventions and expectations about working hours and conditions. Arthur became expert in quick decisions, clearly explained and firmly enforced.

In this busy summer, he found little time to wonder how his daughters were doing, in their first encounter with the wild cottage country south of the construction sites he was visiting.

Actually, Jim Laing had accompanied Bertha and Zoë on the short  ride on the Algoma Eastern Railway, through the rugged country between Sudbury and Georgian Bay. As they came toward the landing, the ferryman called out, "How come you bring two girls, Jim?"

Jim yelled back, "It's all I can afford, so far!"

Zoë, disembarking, was mobbed by Jim's younger sisters and dragged off to see their favourite sights: the tallest pine tree, the hawthorn dell, the bunkhouse, the covered well.

Mrs. Laing took Bertha up to the cottage to help with preparing tea,  while Jim went in search of firewood. The visit to the cottage was off to a good start.

Soon Zoë was involved in all camp activities, including helping with the Monday washing. She grumbled at the assumption that a woman's place was at the washtub while a man's place was on the lake, paddling a canoe. Jim ignored her and took Bertha on a happy exploration of the bay and its rocky cottage countryside.

Back home in Sudbury, the girls' obvious happiness converted Lizzie to the idea that the move north had not been as disastrous as she had feared.

fourteen

Dynamite
Sudbury, 1911–12

Superintendent Smith found it hard to focus on the general needs of his Lake Superior Division. Problems particular to the Sudbury station distracted him. A Toronto-to-Sudbury connection with the westbound transcontinental train from Montreal had been established in 1908, but Torontonians travelling to Vancouver still complained bitterly about switching to westbound trains at ugly Sudbury.

As Arthur had learned, the station had been a point of contention long before he arrived. Ever since the mining boom began, the city had pleaded for a more impressive station reflecting the wealth and business spawned in the Sudbury area. Mayor John McLeod now brought indignation to a head. A very public meeting called for "A.L. Smith, the kingpin of the railway interests here," to present the case to the Canadian Pacific Railway Company for a new, bigger, grander Sudbury station. The editor of the Sudbury *Journal*, who also chaired the high school board, and was a fierce booster of civic pride, caught the city's mood when he thundered, "Consider the local banks, the new brick factory, Eaton's Department store, and the flourishing businessmen such as Frank Cochrane! And then look at the CPR station, still unfinished!"

After the local dignitaries moved on, he gladly welcomed a visit from Jack Hammell, the local businessman who had captured Eola Jaffray's heart. He asked whether Jack had been one of the prospectors who opened up the district for mining in the 1880s. A roar of laughter. "Me a prospector? Going through the bush, boots partly laced, and no hat to keep the little brain from sun rays?" No, he was a promoter, he proclaimed, and about to go back to Toronto to raise money to float another nickel-copper mine northeast of Sudbury.

Arthur decided that he too should take a trip. He would go to Montreal to convince the managers there to authorize construction of a new station for Sudbury, grand enough to please the growing city. It was time, at any rate, for him to accompany Zoë on her own journey, to McGill University in Montreal. She was only sixteen; luckily, she would have at least one good friend there in Dora Braidwood.
Her first letter home announced that she and Dora had quickly found lots of friends among the other young "Freshettes." Her second letter added that she had been elected president of first-year women students at McGill. She and her classmates posed for a picture to appear in the McGill yearbook: the young women who would graduate as "The Class of 1915." Zoë sat in the front row, second from the right.

Bertha, aware that this should have been the beginning of her own graduation year, was left rather desolate. Eola, however, was here in  Sudbury to renew the friendship of their trip to the west. She recruited Bertha for a trip downtown. It was Wednesday—half-holiday for the miners—so the streets were busy, noisy with lumbermen in town to buy supplies and spend a roaring time in the taverns. Railway workers, Italians mostly in this section, blocked the sidewalk as they peered into store windows at an array of goods beyond their power of buying. A few Ojibwas, in from the reserve, slipped through the crowds, followed by their silent wives. Miners, curiously pale in comparison to the Italians and indigenous people, shucked off the tough hours of underground drilling and moved with the swagger of prestige, outfacing all the other labourers in town.

Eola carefully lifted her skirt above the dust and debris swirling around her boots. Bertha, whose skirts had been shortened already in preparation for a visit to McGregor Bay, pulled her hem a notch higher. They were the only young women walking through the downtown area. Eola laughed, "No more chaperones now, eh, Bertha? Remember poor cousin Mearle—how hard she worked to protect us innocents out in Vancouver?" Eola rolled her eyes. "My parents still feel I am walking around too freely," she announced. "But my friend Jack Hammell says the New Woman should hold up her head and stride along wherever she chooses to go."

And here was Bertha's father, crossing the intersection, on his way to the railway station. He reversed his direction and spoke to them. Were the girls on their own here in this district? Bertha answered, "Oh, we're fine, Father!" and Eola interjected, "The New Woman, Cousin Arthur –" But Arthur offered an imperative arm to each of them. It was hard to hold a gentleman's arm and manage at the same time to keep long skirts out of the swirling dust. It was also hard not to gawk at the rollicking scenes on the streets near the taverns.

"We won't tell Mother where I ran into you," Arthur said. He accompanied them back to the Jaffrays' house, then returned to his office. But he chuckled at the girls' spunky conduct. On the whole, he felt that the move to Sudbury was working out well both for himself and his family.

When Jack Hammell came back from Toronto, he announced to the Jaffray family that he intended to marry Eola. To their dismay, Eola announced her equal intention. The Jaffrays called on the Smiths for support: "Eola is much too young!"

Eola played what she saw as a trump card: "Cousin Lizzie, I'm as old as you were when you married Cousin Arthur."

Lizzie said gently, "The real trouble isn't how old you are, but how old Jack is! He must be almost forty!"

To which Eola retorted, "He's thirty-four. And it doesn't matter." The Jaffrays found themselves up against an iron will. So plans were made for a wedding early in 1912, with Bertha as bridesmaid.

The Smiths had joined the small Anglican Church of the Epiphany, in time to learn that the congregation had raised enough funds to build a larger edifice. Sudbury now had a population of 4,150, of whom some 200 were Anglicans. The new enlarged church would celebrate its opening, decorously, next spring, with a choral concert. The Reverend James Boydell heard about Bertha's aspirations as a singer and happily passed along the news to his choirmaster, a fiery Welshman named Llewelyn Davies.

In the first choir practice of the season, Mr. Davies recognized an unusual voice. When Bertha told him shyly about studying with Madame Koestler in Montreal, he invited her to try out for the solo part in next Sunday's anthem. This led quickly to a further request that she participate in a festive Christmas concert at the city hall.

Well before the night of the 1911 Christmas concert, Llewelyn Davies told Bertha that Sudbury was not, in his opinion, ready for Titania's aria. "Something simpler?" Yes, Bertha had learned "The Wings of the Dove," as a possible encore in Montreal. *"Far away, far away would I fly!"* she sang to him, full voice. A sure-fire favourite, he agreed. A good way to end the program.

The Christmas concert turned out to be a total success, thanks to Mr. Davies' coaching and also to an audience of friends and parents who vigorously cheered all the performers. Eola and her friend Jack Hammell came with Jim Laing, hot from his final set of mid-terms at Toronto. For the finale, Bertha stood straight, one hand cupping the other, and her voice soared. *"O, for the wings, for the wings of a dove!"* The applause was undoubtedly heartier than it would have been at the Montreal Ladies' Morning Musicale.

As Bertha moved with her friends toward the exit, she recognized among the audience "the man with five boys to feed," sitting in an aisle seat. She felt a twinge of embarrassment. But he smiled as she passed him and simply said, "You have a wonderful voice, Miss Smith!"

"I do, I do!" Miss Smith thought to herself as she wrapped a silk scarf around her throat before going out into the cool night air. "Not as wonderful as it could be—but good enough for Sudbury!"

She was glad to be swept away to Chez Marie, the respectable restaurant that had coffee and French pastries on offer. Jim hummed an off-key version of "The Wings of the Dove." "You'll be a pretty fat dove if you go on cramming in chocolate éclairs like that, Buffy!" She looked Jim in the eye and picked up another éclair. Llewelyn Davies, passing the table, paused, reached for her hand and kissed it, éclair and all. Jim waited till he was out of earshot. "Good gosh, Buffy!"

Zoë, home for Christmas, brought happy news. She had done well in mid-term exams. And two of the young men in her history class had invited her to join the Young Men's Christian Association, which was eager to welcome young women as adjunct members. Lizzie worried about Zoë's casual shower of references to "Murray and Harry and Edward and Eldon."

March brought the excitements of Eola's formal wedding at the Anglican church. Jack carried his bride away for an unusual honeymoon, on the first of what would be a lifetime of trips into rough mining country. Through North Bay toward Timiskaming and Long Lake; seeing prospects, he told her—copper, nickel, iron, silver, gold—potential wealth everywhere. He brought her back to her parents' home, and left for Toronto, Bay Street, and investors willing to take a chance on him.

But there was other news from Montreal that spring. Distressing news. On April 12, 1912, the "unsinkable" *Titanic* struck an iceberg off the coast of Newfoundland and sank. International news; but for Canada the sinking had extra import. Charles Melville Hays, the dynamic president of the Grand Trunk Railway, and two of his principal assistants had perished in the tragic sea disaster.

For everyone in the railway world, whether employed by the Grand Trunk or by its rivals, the great company seemed to be going down too. Everyone knew about the fragile finances of the Grand Trunk, and no one understood the complexities of Hays' plans for the future. No one had been tapped as heir-apparent for Hays' leadership role.

In the wake of Hays' death and the probability of bankruptcy of his company, questions were raised in Parliament about the future costs of maintaining transcontinental service. As Superintendent of the CPR's Lake Superior Division, A.L. Smith was drawn into official discussions in Montreal about problems on the north shore stretch of track. Hundreds of miles of granite mountains, lakes, and swamps had been half-conquered by the first wave of construction of a single track. Many rough track locations along the route now needed attention. In particular, Superintendent Smith advised his superiors of new local problems:

some of the tracks had been flooded recently in Kenora at the western limit of the Lake Superior Division. They would have to be laid anew. Management suggested that Superintendent Smith had better check the far west stretch of his bailiwick in person.

Arthur planned to take the night train to Kenora, and return to Sudbury by easy stages, performing a rigorous inspection in daytime at each stop along the way back. Since the late Grand Trunk President had set a bad example of not delegating enough responsibility, Arthur deputed some of his local responsibilities to Mickey McNair before departing for the west.

"When you're that far west, why not go on to Winnipeg and visit cousin Mearle?" Lizzie asked, but Kenora was far enough west for Arthur. A note from Lizzie to Mearle, however, brought an offer from James Gordon to arrange special treatment in Port Arthur.

In June, 1912, he settled comfortably into his berth in a Pullman car—one of the first steel sleeping cars in service in Canada, on one of its experimental runs. He breakfasted in an elegant dining car, also among the first in use in this modern year. Very comfortable indeed. He found a similar comfortable modernity in the Tourist Hotel in Kenora where he had made a reservation. He would be saddened to hear, a few months later, that the handsome hotel had burned down. Meanwhile, in the morning he was happy to find that the troublesome Kenora flooding had been dealt with effectively and economically by the local CPR staff. He began his return trip sooner than expected, and in good spirits.

The eastbound train brought him first to Port Arthur. There he found that James Gordon had made good on his promise of help. One of Gordon's associates drove Arthur around the city and its vicinity in a high-toned automobile and offered advice about railway business in western Canada. He declared that the main impediment to Canadian Pacific success there was not the Grand Trunk Pacific Railway, but the new Canadian Northern Railway that had been pushed across the prairies by the Ontario entrepreneurs William Mackenzie and Donald Mann. The CNoR was the preferred carrier of wheat from the prairies to the head of

Lake Superior. At present, he added, steamships, rather than railways, offered the best and cheapest transportation from Port Arthur to the eastern and European markets.

Arthur visited the wharves and saw that the bulk of western wheat was indeed moving, not via the wild north shore of Lake Superior with the problematic CPR, but more directly eastward by steamship, expeditiously and cheaply, to Sault Ste. Marie, where Superior flowed into Lake Huron. The Canadian Pacific Railway obviously had everything to gain by pushing ahead with track and grade improvements along the north shore.

The trip back to Sudbury was slow enough to give Arthur time to sort out these ideas and bits of advice. Since steam locomotives required frequent stops in this harsh terrain to take on water, there were many local stops. Trains required crew changes, coal replenishment, and general servicing 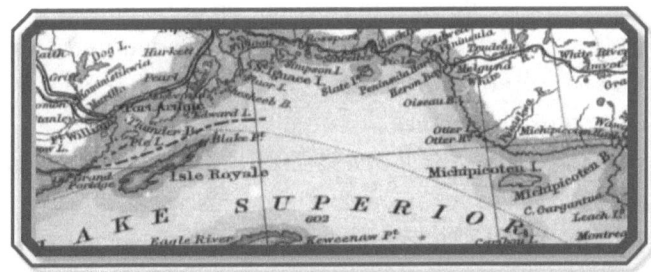 every 125 miles or so, and "division" points had been established at roughly these intervals. So at Nipigon, Schreiber, and White River, Arthur stepped down from the train for a slow and thorough inspection.

The landscape was bleak but the countryside was stirring with potential growth and development. Trackmen worked strenuously to install or lengthen sidings and strengthen bridges. Most importantly, they worked on grade improvement. Labourers heaved finished lumber into place as ties, ahead of other men carrying lengths of steel to be pounded onto that base. Arthur watched the survey gangs where construction engineers worked with transits and chains to check levels and explore the best locations for the realigned tracks. He admitted to himself that he felt less happy watching men placing sticks of dynamite where cliffs of stone blocked the way.

Near Schreiber, he met his old acquaintance Dan Hillman, who was in the process of directing the dynamiting there. Arthur watched—from a prudent distance. Dynamiting over, he offered Dan congratulations and suggested that next time he travelled east, he should visit the Smiths' Sudbury home.

Not possible, Dan told him. He had orders to report to Montreal for a stint in the Chief Engineer's office, as soon as the present tunnel work was completed. He must regretfully decline Arthur's invitation. "But please tell your daughter how much I enjoyed hearing her sing at the Christmas concert."

Arthur sighed. His daughter had a fine voice according to experts but she needed more training than Sudbury could offer. Dan tactfully dropped the talk of Bertha's dilemma, and switched to praise of Arthur's western sortie. "It's a good thing you're making this trip, A.L. It will give you weapons to fight the politicians—and our own management—if they threaten to slow our progress on this stretch of track." He laughed. "We need a bit of diplomatic dynamite to stir up support for construction like this." He gestured at the scene in front of them, as another explosion shattered a stone bastion.

Arthur arrived back in Sudbury, ready to go on to Montreal to make an urgent case for improving the track north of Lake Superior. The Canadian Pacific must not lose the transcontinental battle for western business. He would use the strongest possible terms in his report to the Montreal headquarters. "Diplomatic dynamite"—he smiled at memory of his friend Dan's words. The Grand Trunk was in tragic disarray. The Canadian Pacific must take advantage of the moment and blast ahead.

fifteen

Junction
McGregor Bay, 1912–13

By the summer of 1912, monumental carloads of grain from the west could move through the district north of Lake Superior. This largest grain movement in the British Empire transported 80 million dollars' worth of freight, all told. Passenger traffic through Sudbury amounted to another 32 million dollars' worth. Besides the ever-growing transcontinental business, the CPR catered to nearby mining and smelting enterprises whose private tracks joined the main line in Sudbury.

Consequently, access to the city by train now entailed penetrating a tangled junction of tracks belonging to numerous smaller railways. Several local mines depended on one such set of tracks. The Algoma Eastern Railway, originally named the Manitoulin and North Shore Railway, had started running into Sudbury in 1900, bringing supplies and personnel. This little railway had no station in the city. Instead, its officers managed a complicated transport system from a boxcar located at the Elm Street crossing on the CPR line. Jim Laing was one of many young mining engineers who took the Algoma Eastern to get to his new job at the British American Nickel Corporation building, down at the old Murray Mine site. Here prospectors had discovered the huge vein of ore that burgeoned into a great mining enterprise. Beyond the mines, the Algoma Eastern meandered southward past McGregor Bay and then to Manitoulin Island. The little railway was a local joke in Sudbury, but Arthur, as Superintendent of the Lake Superior Division, worried that the Grand Trunk might take a sudden interest in the Algoma Eastern, seeing it as a potential link through Sault Ste. Marie to mid-western American rail lines and markets.

Arthur traced the crossings of this and other lines as he paced along the trail of crushed stone that buttressed the CPR main tracks. The interchanges wove a complicated web. Back in his office, Arthur looked at an example of even greater complexity in a photograph of a German junction. Germany seemed to be stealing an advantage over other modern nations in railroading, as in many other matters.

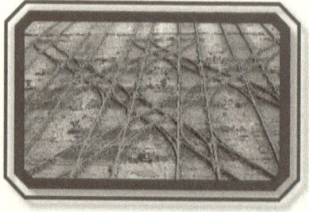

Arthur's daughters were travelling at this moment via the Algoma Eastern for a second visit to McGregor Bay. Cottage life suited Zoë, safely back from her first year at McGill. She and Jessie Laing, now a student at the University of Toronto, had maintained a happy correspondence all year. Soon they were in hilarious cahoots at the camp, getting up comic skits in the evenings by the bonfire. Outfitted in outrageous camp trousers and shirts, they blasted the adults into acceptance of modern women's rights.

The cottage held no such appeal to Bertha at the outset. This spring Jim and Bea and her other classmates had graduated from the University of Toronto. Regret fell heavily on her. "Come on, slowpoke!" Jim cried. "Come for a canoe ride. No time to waste!" She followed him down over the rocks to the dock and stepped gingerly into the canoe. Moments later, she was not just trying to look as if she were enjoying herself. She was indeed delighting in this sunlit day, the quiet water, and Jim's steady dip and swing of the paddle.

Jim, graduated as a full-fledged mining engineer, had found a promising position at the Nickel Corporation. Unfortunately, this job meant he would have only a week's holiday this year. He paused, paddle poised, then grinned and declared, "But such is life!" Bertha returned to shore feeling that life, such as it was, was not entirely bad after all.

When the summer ended, local dignitaries had a new axe to grind with the CPR Division Superintendent. They urged him to authorize a new section of rail to replace the oldest tracks in the area. The original cutting, dynamited out of stone outcropping by CPR navvies in the 1880s, had created an awkward angular access to Sudbury from Ottawa and Montreal. But the workers there had uncovered the richest source of ore in the north. Discovery of the great lode had led to a "rush" bringing growth and prosperity to Sudbury in the last century. Now the civic leaders, as well as prospectors and promoters, saw the old narrow rail cutting as a misfortune, a restraint on further findings. Maybe creating a new, easier access from the east would also reveal another big lode like the 1883 find! Arthur, straining to conclude the track improvements far west of the city, could only hope that Christmas would take Sudbury councillors' minds off that notion.

Christmas brought a bagful of letters. Lizzie looked up from a card from Mearle Gordon, with a question. "That young Winnipeg doctor that was so keen on you, Bertha. What was his name?"

Bertha said "Craig McLaren" quietly, and Lizzie, equally quietly, passed along news. Mearle's letter mentioned that the young doctor had become engaged to one of Jim Gordon's cousins. Bertha had nothing to say to that. Two days later she was astonished to receive a letter with the once familiar handwriting. Craig wrote with a second version of the news of his engagement. His letter ended, surprisingly, *"I must tell you, Bertha, that an old song still runs in my mind: 'You are neater, and you're sweeter than a full-blown rose...'"* A funny kind of letter to be sent by a man engaged to another young lady, Bertha thought. He had better settle down soon! She pushed the letter into a drawer.

She had been working with Llewelyn Davies as voice coach all fall, and was now helping him organize the next Christmas concert. This time, with Mr. Davies' encouragement, she would perform her "Titania" aria. The audience included not only Jim Laing but also his two new friends, Roddy Morton and Ken Moore, recent engineering graduates from Queen's University who had come north for mining experience. They listened politely to Bertha's performance, perhaps a little overawed. They enjoyed much more heartily the humorous version of "A Partridge in a Pear Tree" that she offered as an encore.

Zoë was in the audience too, home for Christmas, full of happy stories of her second year at McGill. Her parents were less than pleased when she announced that she would not be coming straight home after

her spring exams. She had enrolled for the YMCA leadership camp in Muskoka. "She is spreading her wings, Mother," Arthur said.

Lizzie answered, "I would prefer it if she spread them again at McGregor Bay."

In the early spring of 1913, local political and business leaders again paid Superintendent Arthur Lloyd Smith a formal visit. They were delighted that the CPR had erected a fine new edifice to serve as the divisional office building, and had left the smaller 1907 station intact as an adjunct. Sitting solidly at the southeast corner of the downtown business district, the

long-desired new station was a source of civic pride. And the completion of the new complex at the Sudbury divisional point affirmed the CPR's pivotal role in the city's economic life.

The whole Smith family turned out for the official opening of the handsome building. Each member privately dreamed of standing on the wide new platform sometime soon, waiting to start on new travel ventures. For Arthur, the building also represented the culmination of his work in the north. Sudbury was now perceived as a major junction in the Canadian rail system.

For Sudbury's young folk, it was more likely a horse and buggy, rather than a newfangled automobile, that came to a stop at the local junctions—the level crossings where the roads ran over the train lines. Jim and his friends Rod and Ken invested in a lively horse and

a smart rig and took turns driving their young lady friends around the dusty roads near Sudbury on the weekends, until happy summertime came again. Then Jim left the horse and buggy for his friends and headed to McGregor Bay, accompanying Bertha and Zoë.

One evening as the canoe drifted over quiet waters, Bertha asked him, "Have you ever heard an old song that goes like this: *'You're neater and you're sweeter Than a full-blown rose'?*"

"Sure," said Jim, "That's from 'Maisy'—it's an old vaudeville song." He sang the rest of the song in a not-so-tuneful voice:

> *Come, dear, I'm here*
> *Waiting just for you!*
> *If you miss me,*
> *Come and kiss me!*

With considerable danger to the canoe's stability, Jim acted on the song's suggestion.

Of all the season's photos, the favourite proved to be one of Bertha laughing with Jim.

When autumn came, she went back to serious work on voice development under Llewelyn Davies' direction. Jim spent his spare time devising ways to attach gliders to the wheels of his buggy so that it could be converted into a winter conveyance. He worked alone. Rod and Ken had lost interest in sharing their weekends with him. They had returned to Queen's University for a fall homecoming weekend and come back, engaged, each of them, to a Queen's girl graduate. In mid-December, Ken Morton married his Alice, and Roddy Moore his Mab. Jim, the best man, confused everyone with a rambling toast to the "brideses."

Zoë came home for Christmas full of tales of her third-year classes at McGill University. She had enrolled in the popular course given by the celebrated Stephen Leacock, who brought his famous wit to his lectures on economics and political science. Zoë spent endless hours studying theories about supply and demand, labour relations, and statistical probability, joined with other endless hours chuckling over Leacock's current bestselling book, *Sunshine Sketches of a Little Town*. To her delight, she was photographed with the famous professor.

Bertha found the "Stevie-worship" a little hard to bear. Never mind: the 1913 Christmas concert was drawing near and she would be singing her new solo there. Eola and Jack Hammell would be back in Sudbury to hear it. They had moved to a big house in the Rosedale area of Toronto: Jack was emerging as a major entrepreneur in the mining world.

Another former acquaintance would be present too, though Bertha was unaware of it. Her father had neglected to mention that a wire had come from his friend Dan Hillman, saying he had completed a northern survey and was now on his way to CPR headquarters in Montreal. He would drop in to see the Smiths, "around the time of Miss Bertha's recital." He quietly joined Arthur and Lizzie and Eola and Jack in the middle of the hall.

Bertha's younger friends occupied the two front rows. They looked forward to her performance, though they were secretly afraid it might be a little highfalutin. Yes, she did indeed offer an operatic aria this year, the "Mirror Song" from Gounod's *Faust*. Holding a small mirror as a theatrical prop, she released the fuller, higher voice that was developing under Llewelyn Davies' tutelage *"O chérie! Tu es si belle en ce miroir!"*

The audience seemed dazed by the artistry and ardour in her voice. But perhaps it was not a sufficiently lady-like song? Her encore was much easier to enjoy. From Gilbert and Sullivan's popular *Mikado*, Bertha sang a young woman's mischievous boast, equating herself laughingly to "the sun's celestial highness." She began the song quietly, a little humour in her voice and her stance.

> *The sun, whose rays are all ablaze with ever-living glory,*
> *Does not deny his majesty—he scorns to tell a story!*
> *But fierce and bold, in fiery gold, he glories all effulgent –*

And then—full voice—with surprising power blended with sweetness, the claim rang out:

> *I mean to rule the earth, as he the sky –*
> *We really know our worth, the sun and I.*

The audience roared approval. This year there were bouquets for the singer as she took her final bow and swept down the stair from the stage into the audience. Bertha slid into a seat beside her parents. She said hello to Dan, who was sitting between them. He smiled, and then, suddenly serious, asked her, "You really do know your worth, don't you?"

Caught unaware, without her usual guard of modesty about her gift, she admitted the charge. "Yes, I do!" Then she snapped back, "I bet you are pretty ambitious too, aren't you?"

She caught a quick flash of light from the grey eyes watching her. "Yes, I am." And he told her he was leaving the next day for Montreal, to accept an appointment as Assistant to the Chief Engineer of the CPR. He did not tell her that he planned to be Chief Engineer himself someday.

Lizzie broke in to say, "You should go back to your friends, Bertha. They are getting impatient!" Bertha smiled again and left to join Jim, with Ken and Alice, and Roddy and Mab, for a riotous reception and a double order of éclairs at Chez Marie. Bertha's spirits rose with the thought of making friends with the cheerful young brides now happily settling in to life in Sudbury.

sixteen

Crossing
Canada, 1914

Most of the older Canadian cities, like European ones, had grown around a waterway. Sudbury, like most newer towns in America, had grown  around a railway line. Consequently, most north-south streets in the emerging city created hazards when they crossed the central railway tracks. Early in 1914, the Sudbury Council, nudged by the Division Superintendent, installed signs at central level crossings. They followed the national signage standards: two boards, one marked "RAILWAY," the other, "CROSSING," were nailed across each other at a 60-degree angle. The Council decided to also erect pendulum-swinging, high-bell-dinging "wigwags." Arthur rejoiced at the sight and sound of  a device that could have saved many an earlier train wreck.

Another cooperative action resulted in the 1914 construction of a handsome ticket and telegraphy building, north of the railway station on Elgin Street—an appropri-  ate monument to the change and growth in the communication system that had given Arthur his start, and to civic pride in Sudbury's progress.

Zoë returned home from college, but not until after spending a happy time at the YMCA camp in the Laurentians. She told her parents that it had featured Bible study groups and evening meetings in the open-air chapel—as well as boating trips, walks, sports, and a "stunt day." Her parents were pleased, though glad to welcome her back to a less colourful Sudbury.

In July the two sisters went to the Laings' cottage. Jim swept Bertha away for the first canoe ride around the lake. Without preamble, he told her, "I guess we should get engaged this summer, Buffy, so we can be married around Thanksgiving, before the heavy snows begin." Then the paddle dipped and swung, dipped and swung, steady and strong, as the canoe slipped around the point of land. Finally Jim pulled the paddle out of the water and laid it across his knees. "Say something, Buffy!"

"I mustn't cry," Bertha thought. But tears were sliding, seeping, spilling. She turned her face down so that the brim of her hat would hide them. They had known each other for five years, and they were both twenty-four years old now. He had a good job and a promising future. She had no business crying.

A quick dip of the paddle pulled them away from the shore line. "I guess I said that the wrong way!" Jim laughed. "Come on, Buffy. Say something. Use your famous voice! Sing to me if that's any easier. Or just nod."

The brim of the hat moved slowly, slightly, up and down. That was good enough for Jim; the paddle powered in with vigour. "We'll go tell the family."

There were happy tears from Mrs. Laing, and romantic tears from Jim's sisters, overcome by dreams of engagement parties and a stylish wedding. Bertha felt she was crossing an invisible line between her family and Jim's. "You must speak to Bertha's father," Mrs. Laing said.

"Oh, I already did that," Jim said airily. "He seemed encouraging I think, but he was busy so I didn't take much of his time."

Arthur had ambivalent feelings about the young man's request to consider himself engaged to marry Bertha. A good-looking young man, undoubtedly with brains enough to graduate from the University of Toronto with an engineering degree, a youth from a nice family, but somehow lacking the gravity of Bertha's earlier suitor, Dr. McLaren. What did Lizzie think?

Lizzie thought Bertha would not likely meet many other eligible men here in Sudbury; her loneliness had been a worry for some time now. And Jim was a nice young man.

No one asked Zoë's opinion. She spent a solitary hour perched on a rock at the shore before coming in to the cottage to join in the congratulations. She privately felt that Jim was gauche, and she looked forward to her own coming year at McGill, where presumably battalions of more sophisticated men were waiting. Meantime the summer would be pleasanter if Bertha stopped moping about her precious voice and baffled ambitions: Jim looked like a good remedy for melancholy.

In August, that summer world ended.

A faraway Austrian archduke was assassinated by some Serbian or other—and somehow the network of alliances in Europe drew tragically tight. Germany invaded Belgium, and Great Britain, as Belgium's ally, declared war. The newspapers shouted the story of the British Expeditionary Force embarking for France within a week, preparing to march north to the Belgian border to face the German army: Bismarck, the warmonger! The Kaiser, the Boche, the Hun! Of course, if Britain was at war, so were all the members of the British Empire, the colonies, the protectorates, and the far-flung dominions, including the Dominion of Canada.

An alert came from the Canadian Pacific Railway headquarters: Sudbury must be ready for a surge of troop trains from the west: men joining up in Alberta, Saskatchewan, Manitoba, and British Columbia would be rushed through basic training, and immediately transported toward the eastern embarkation ports: Montreal, Quebec City, Saint John. Sudbury would also be immediately involved in the local gathering of war materials. A.L. Smith, as Superintendent of Lake Superior Division, must expedite swift forwarding of mineral and wood products essential for British war equipment. A double challenge; yet he felt his work was hardly significant, compared to the terrible battles already being fought on the far-off borders of Belgium and France.

A second, more personal alert reached James Laing and his friends Roderick Morton and Kenneth Moore. The Canadian Engineering Institute sent each of them a letter, urging them to join the Royal Canadian Engineers and prepare to go overseas at once. Their expertise in dynamiting and drilling, acquired in their mining apprenticeship, was essential for modern war. Once they passed the physical examination, they would be commissioned as officers and put in charge of a group of sappers attached to the British Expeditionary Force.

Jim burst in with this news when Bertha was teaching scales to a young student. Behind Jim came Rod and Ken. "We're going to Toronto," they announced in chorus. "To the recruiting centre." They explained to Bertha and her goggle-eyed pupil that they hoped the war wouldn't be over before they got overseas. Jim paused to say, "We'll be back before spring. Then we can talk about getting married and all that!" The three excited young men gave Bertha and her little pupil a salute and wheeled away, presumably to bring their news to Alice and Mab.

Off they went for Toronto and enlistment. Soon they sent back photos taken at the training camp in the Toronto Exhibition grounds. The picture of their smiling faces was examined with pride and secret misgivings.

A.L. Smith had no time for vague misgivings. He worked at expediting the massive movement of men through his district to all the training camps, and from his region in Canada to the war front overseas. By September, 1914, large contingents came in troop trains to northern Ontario from the prairies and the far west.

Fitting these trains into the regularly scheduled timetable was difficult enough. But would it be possible to avoid train wrecks in this time of confusion and change? On the national railway line between

 Kenora and Sudbury, there were innumerable dangerous crossings. Small spur lines from the mines and the lumber camps crossed the main line at short irregular intervals. Between Kenora and Port Arthur the map showed 19 whistle stops; 39 between Port Arthur and White River at the Algoma district line; and 39 more between White River and Sudbury.

In remote areas like the half-empty land north of Lake Superior, signalmen had been reluctant to accept the shift from the telegraph to the telephone. Today, considering the confusions in this war situation, that shift was imperative. The time-honoured telegraph would not be rapid enough to alert main-line engine drivers of unexpected dangers when trains from the mining and lumber spurs came to cross the main tracks.

In restless energy Arthur visited the outlying parts of his enlarged district, stopping at the small railway settlements where he could find overnight accommodation in small hotels, or shacks, or boxcars pulled off into sidings. At every crossing he checked the signal systems. Was the local agent ready to warn of sudden changes in scheduling whenever troop trains disrupted regular service? Everywhere, he tried to hasten the shift to the use of the telephone because of the new urgencies of wartime train movement.

Back in Sudbury, wire messages from overseas brought the incomprehensible news of the defeat of the British and French armies in the battle of Mons. In that embattled village, British and French armies struggled desperately to prevent German forces from invading France. Imaginable or not, the British Expeditionary Force was pushed back, inch by bloody inch along the Marne River. The French allies and British armies retreated toward an imperiled Paris. By September fourth, the advancing German army was barely thirty miles from Paris.

Nowhere in Canada was this disaster more strongly felt than in Montreal. Zoë, arriving back at McGill to begin her second year, found a war-centred campus. She took a photo of her friend, Harry Beatty, in his

Canadian Officers' Corps uniform, standing alone on the campus. By November she could "snap" a whole contingent of student-soldiers, marching in a quite impressive drill on campus. Normal social life withered: no dances, few club meetings, and very few sporting events. Most male students were exhaust-

ed by the combination of military drills with the strain of deciding whether and when to "join up."

In November, Jim, Rod, and Ken sent news of their move to training camp in New Brunswick. Next they wrote that they would be crossing to England, without embarkation leave. Then their letters stopped throughout a frightening fortnight. Eventually word came: they were camped in Longmoor in Hampshire, under the command of the British Royal Engineers. Their letters, although censored by superior officers, managed to suggest that their training was not furnishing them with new ideas about ways to set explosives in bridges and fortifications. Instead, they were learning how to command the sappers who would be digging trenches under fire. Both the Allies and their enemies were settling in for a war of attrition, small sorties, and brief forays from the network of trenches across the northeastern part of France.

Recruiting was going apace in Sudbury. Arthur's friend Dan Hillman had returned briefly from his job in Montreal as Assistant Engineer of Construction in order to rally railway workers into signing up for a special battalion he was helping to raise. In August, 1914, on the first day of the war, he and his boss, Colin Ramsey, the Chief Construction Engineer of the Canadian Pacific Railway, had suggested to their employer that troops in France and Belgium would need rapidly built railway lines, whether they were advancing or retreating. Who could do this front-line job of construction better than men from the Canadian frontier? The CPR officials agreed. By the end of the year the British government concurred, and authorized the formation of a corps of such men. With the blessing of Canadian and railway authorities, an informal recruiting office opened in November at the new Sudbury telegraphy building. Labourers on the Superior line poured in, eager to join the Canadian Overseas Railway Construction Corps, in hope of going overseas to construct, repair, and maintain railways near the Allied front lines.

Dan Hillman, now commissioned as a lieutenant, dropped in to Arthur's office with news of their numbers. The Corps would consist of two companies, each enrolling two hundred and fifty men; they would muster in St. John, New Brunswick, ready to go overseas early in 1915. Shortly after hearing this news from Dan, Arthur told him in return that the CPR had instructed every General Superintendent to appoint recruiting officers in his district. Arthur's appointees would find northern men other than those railway workers already signed up for the Corps. The list of volunteers included several Ojibway men from the nearest reserve, guaranteed to be good fighters.

In Montreal, most of the young men Zoë and her friends had known in their first years at McGill had left by Christmas, 1914, to join the army or navy, carrying with them a promise that places would be held for them when they returned. Many of Zoë's women friends found their way into areas of study previously closed to them. With particular daring, Eleanor Percival, Jessie Boyd, and Glad Storey demanded admission into pre-medical laboratories in hematology. "Well—the lab spaces are here and empty," a laboratory assistant grumbled. "You ladies might as well occupy them." For her part, Zoë was able to move from a rather dull political science course into a smaller advanced senior honours class. Here, too, spaces opened up as young men dropped out of college to enlist.

The Sudbury church choir that Bertha belonged to was temporarily disbanded: Llewelyn Davies had decamped for Wales to join the Welsh Guards. Bertha and the two young brides, Mab and Alice, joined the Red Cross recruits like Lizzie and her friends and began to roll bandages, knit rough wool into khaki balaclavas, designed to protect soldiers' faces in the cold winter overseas, and sew little dresses for evacuees from Belgium. It was quite a change from embroidering monograms on linen tablecloths for a trousseau.

As Christmas approached, Sudbury's school principal invited Bertha to organize as well as perform in the annual concert. Bertha offered "The Wings of a Dove" as her solo, the words familiar now to her audience: *"Far away, far away I would fly!"* Instead of an encore, she began a sing-song. Men, women, and children first joined in a Christmas carol dear to all of them, "Away in a Manger." Then Bertha led them to a different "Away": a song, from overseas. Jim, Roddy, and Ken had made a tour of London music halls on their brief leave, before crossing the channel to France. They had sent home sheet-music copies of the popular songs they heard there. So now Sudbury sang, quietly and wistfully:

> *There's a silver lining,*
> *Through the dark clouds shining,*
> *Turn the dark clouds inside out*
> *Till the boys come home.*

s e v e n t e e n

Rails
World at War, 1915

Troop trains roared through Sudbury early in 1915, carrying recruits from the western provinces toward the eastern seaboard. In Vancouver, Calgary, Regina, and Winnipeg, a generation of Canadians dominated by immigrants from the British Isles had mustered to fight along with "the dear old mother country." All Canadian schoolchildren still sang imperial British songs like "The thistle, shamrock, rose entwine the Maple Leaf forever!" Arthur Lloyd Smith, son of a soldier from Yorkshire, recognized his patriotic duty as a British Canadian to facilitate the movement eastward of modern would-be fighters. He disrupted regular schedules, employed extra trainmen, and disregarded the difference between day and night to aid the flow of manpower.

A photograph arrived in a letter for Arthur from overseas, show-ing the officers of the new Canadian Overseas Railway Construction Corps in Longmoor Camp, Hampshire, England. King George V had come to inspect the corps of two companies, each consisting of 254 men, as they prepared to cross the English Channel and go to work on the Belgian Front. Arthur's friend Dan, who had been promoted to the rank of Captain, appeared seated in the centre of the first row, looking off to the right.

Arthur's response to Dan's letter was easy to write. He knew that news of remaining construction gangs north of Lake Superior would be welcome. He passed along word of a visit from Harry McLean, now the major contractor for improving the CPR passage through rocky northern terrain. Arthur made a good story of Harry's familiar roars of wrath over his difficulties getting steel rails and stone ballast and wooden ties because of the competing demands of the armed forces. He knew Dan had a better insight than Harry into the limitation of CPR power to facilitate local construction problems. "The war, you know. . ." Writing a long letter to Dan was almost as good as engaging in the conversations they both used to enjoy, first at White River, and later in Sudbury. Writing easily to a friend was an improvement over talking to local Sudbury authorities about why the CPR placed local needs of new spur lines low on the list of priorities. "The war, you know . . ."

Dan's letter to Arthur included another one for Bertha, which her father passed along to her with a chuckle. It included heavy blackouts of censored details, but its tone was light. *"Dear Miss Bertha: I hope that the war has not silenced your voice! What about your ambition? Still strong, I hope, war or no war.* ▆▆▆ *At least the guns are silent this afternoon, in* ▆▆▆ *Your friend, Dan Hillman."* Bertha responded to the note Dan had addressed to her with an attempt at a humorous report on the Christmas concert. But she found no way to answer, humorously or otherwise, his comments on her voice. There was no effulgence in her career plans this winter.

It was a different situation for Zoë at McGill. She and Dora Braidwood had decided to enrol next fall in the McGill Faculty of Education.  Because of the exodus of male teachers into the armed forces, future teaching positions were guaranteed for them. Comfortable news, but not as exciting as the future possibilities opening to seven of their other graduating friends. Having completed pre-medical requirements, these seven young women now held high hopes of being accepted into the McGill Medical School—again because so many male pre-meds had joined up. Meanwhile the young women of the class of 1915 moved through the May sunshine, gowned and hooded, each with a university diploma in hand.

Zoë's family travelled to Montreal to join the celebrations. Lizzie and Bertha relished the quick way Montreal people walked, the stylish outfits worn by the women in the hotel and on the downtown sidewalks, the range of choices in restaurants, and the accompanying sparkle of overheard conversation from other diners, war or no war.

For Arthur, dropping in to visit friends and colleagues at Windsor Station, a different side of Montreal was manifest: a mood of tension and frustration as the world moved toward the disturbing end of its first year of war. News of the horrors of trench warfare was now augmented by reports of something worse: the nightmare of troops being assaulted with mustard gas, foul clouds seeping across the chewed-up fields along the Belgian Front.

Officials in the CPR's Montreal headquarters called Arthur in to confer over a different issue. The work of the CORCC and other railway troops overseas depended on their receiving steady shipments of supplies. They needed rails, preferably steel, and 40 foot in length. They also needed fishplates, about 15 inches long, to hold every two lengths of rail together. The bolts to fix the fishplates to the joined rail ends

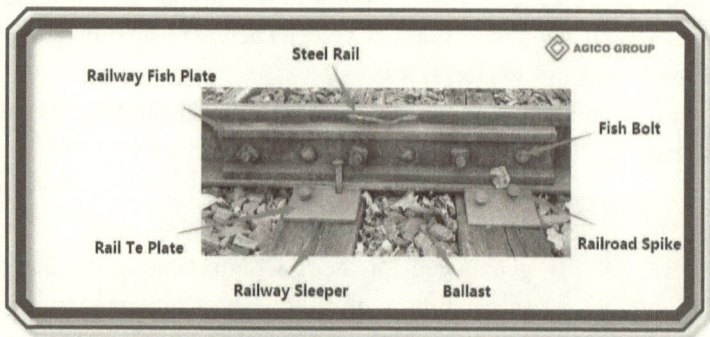

would slide through the holes and be tightened with the nuts to prevent complete separation of the rails under sudden impact. Next, to fix the rails to the wooden ties, they needed tie plates and spikes. All these elements, unlike the rails, were still made of iron. All were essential overseas and it fell to the CPR to assemble them and expedite their passage. Arthur Smith was assigned a new double role: to find new sources of rail materials in his district, and to assert priority for the gondola cars carrying the construction goods through the region he supervised.

The first of these jobs was unexpectedly difficult. The nearest steel manufacturer in the area was Algoma Steel in Sault Ste. Marie, but it had already converted much of its operation into manufacturing artillery shells. Algoma Steel also faced diminishing supplies of iron as old nearby mines began to run out of ore. Other Ontario steel manufacturers, also commissioned by the government to shift into the production of ammunition parts, had nothing in the way of track materials to offer. This problem could grow in significance as the war went on. Arthur found an immediate solution by ordering the tearing up of old steel rails from abandoned CPR siding lines north of Lake Superior. But this resource offered only small pickings.

CNoR & GTP Mainlines
Edmonton, Alta. to Mt. Robson, B.C. 1910 - 1917

Arthur looked hungrily at the map of two rival lines farther west in Canada. The Grand Trunk and the Canadian Northern Railways ran closely parallel from Edmonton almost to the border between Alberta and British Columbia—and most of those two tracks were unused. Devout CPR employee that he was, he mused that surely one or the other could be torn up to create usable rails for the overseas construction people.

Compared to the difficulty of finding rails, the job of organizing a series of gondola cars to carry them from the far west was easy. So enough rail materials to make up a small trainload of gondolas moved eastward from Sudbury by the end of June.

In July, a wire came from Arthur's youngest brother Harry in Edmonton, announcing that he was en route to the war front. Harry Batoche Smith was years younger than Arthur. In a formal family portrait taken in the 1880s, Harry appeared as a very small boy steadied by his tall older brother. Now he was old enough—and young enough—to enlist. In November 1914 he had joined the 49th Battalion, Edmonton Regiment.

He would embark with them for Great Britain in June, 1915, to serve as part of the 7th Infantry Brigade, 3rd Canadian Division, in France and Flanders. Harry's troop train would be going through Toronto in a few days, the wire announced, and he hoped to have a few minutes to visit his family at the station.

Arthur quickly ordered a train pass so that he could go from Sudbury to Toronto, and exchanged telegraphs with his father, arranging to pick up his parents and take them to the station for the brief reunion. In the Toronto Union station, train cars of the Grand Trunk Pacific bringing troops from the west paused to give a brief time for visits with friends and relatives before moving on to Halifax for embarkation. Arthur, with his father and mother and sister, was among the crowd. Harry's visit proved to be awkward and intense. Arthur was tormented by the thought that he had virtually lost touch with this youngest brother,  and racked by consciousness of his own failure to follow in their father's military footsteps.

Back in Sudbury the city fathers had turned the biggest room in the town hall into a work place where the women could do the urgent war work requested by the Red Cross. Rod Moore's bride, Mab, who was managing to maintain herself in Sudbury on a government fund for wives of soldiers overseas, still joined Bertha and Lizzie in their work. Ken Morton's bride, Alice, had yielded to her parents' pleas and gone back to Napanee "for the duration." Hand-rolling bandages led to hand-packing a mixture of medical supplies for shipping overseas along the endangered lines to hospitals in England and France. Later in the spring, the supplies began going by rail to new destinations in Canada, as wounded men began to arrive home in the returning hospital ships.

It was August before the women's Red Cross work was interrupted by the usual visit to McGregor Bay. This year Mrs. Laing had urged Lizzie and Arthur to come too. Lizzie was looking rather frail and gaunt. She had been feeling short of breath lately, and the vigorous life at the cottage was a bit too much for her. Still, she was willing to take the Algoma Eastern train down to McGregor Bay with Bertha and Arthur.

They posed at the water's edge together. Lizzie felt that her parents' presence here might make the visit a little less sad for Bertha, who would no doubt be missing Jim more strongly in this place of happy memories.

Instead of feeling romantically nostalgic, however, Bertha was secretly finding it difficult to play the role of putative daughter-in-law. Nothing was that clearly settled; no formal engagement, no ring—and no very romantic letters forthcoming, though Jim signed all his brief notes, "Your loving Jim."

That summer at McGregor Bay was a strange, man-less time.

In the fall of 1915, Zoë returned to Toronto, secured a room in the YWCA building on Elm Street, and registered at the Toronto Normal School. She was determined, like her friend Dora, to become a public school teacher. By October, though, Normal School classes had become more and more tiresome. "How to clean the blackboard brush," and "How to write on the board without turning your back on the class"—piffle, all of it, in Zoë's opinion. As for the practice-teaching experiences, the classrooms seemed to be filled with too many noisy, silly, or stupid children. When Dora

wrote from Montreal that she was finding real pleasure in teaching, Zoë recognized herself as a square peg in a round hole—a new sensation for a usually triumphant young woman. She wrote home that she was not at all sure she wanted to be a teacher.

Her father had more urgent things to think about. News came that some of the rails he had dispatched had been used to construct tracks just fifteen miles behind the front lines at Ypres. More were desperately needed. It was growing ever harder to find new rails or to scrounge old ones.

At this point, without warning, he was notified of an imminent change of jobs. The personnel officer in Montreal wired the Company's decision that the end of his time as Superintendent of the Superior Division centred in Sudbury was near. On January 1, 1916, he was to be named Superintendent of the whole Ontario Division, with headquarters in Toronto. The present holder of that position had left for overseas service. Arthur was directed to come to Montreal headquarters for a full explanation of what the change of responsibilities entailed.

He went home to tell the news to Lizzie and Bertha. "I've got my walking papers, my dears," he said with a smile. "They want me to move into another position."

Lizzie dropped into the nearest chair. "No, Arthur—surely not!"

He hurried to tell her that it was Toronto, this time—the place they had all regretted leaving; the city they had spoken about so often with longing. But for Lizzie the thought of moving again was literally shocking. She sat down abruptly. "Something's the matter."

The something turned out to be a serious pain, a sense of tightening in her chest. Arthur cried to Bertha, "Run to Dr. Howey's house!" and Bertha scuttled around the corner, to the side door, the entry to the doctor's office. Within minutes Dr. Howey was at Lizzie's side, feeling her pulse, watching the signs that the pain was subsiding. "Angina" was his quick diagnosis, and he offered reassurance. The pain was a warning, an alert to remind a middle-aged person that she should take it easy, avoid stress and tension. Arthur ruefully told Dr. Howey in confidence how difficult that might be, since the family faced an immediate and trying change. The doctor shook his head, then wrote a prescription for nitroglycerine—"Perfectly safe, been in use for over twenty years, won't reverse the damage to the heart but will decrease the intensity of pain if she takes a pill when it recurs." Meantime, rest and relax.

Not till after two days of rest and relaxation did Lizzie say, "All right, Arthur. Toronto."

eighteen

Tunnelling
Ontario, 1916

Unscheduled hospital trains and groups of returning wounded but ambulant soldiers arriving from overseas challenged Arthur's managerial skills during his first days as Superintendent of the Ontario Division. He had to create innovative ways of handling new east-to-west traffic through Toronto and other provincial centres including London, Peterborough, and Ottawa, in these distressing days in the second year of the Great War.

Ottawa needed quick attention for a second reason. Smooth and efficient travel in and out of the national capital city was essential for members of Parliament, Cabinet ministers, and political consultants, whether Parliament was in session or not. In wartime, rail travel to and from Ottawa had to be readily available. Early in January, 1916, Arthur travelled from Toronto to Ottawa via Smiths Falls, tabulating problems on this vital route, newly under his direction. In the process he picked up news of national importance.

People were talking about a growing number of wartime regulations passing through committees, caucuses, and full sessions of Parliament. Like everyone in the railway world, he was particularly interested in one motion currently under discussion. Parliament had established a Royal Commission to consider the possibility of nationalizing the Canadian railways, as a protection of essential transportation in wartime. Talk about this was rife, both on and off the trains. What did it mean? Did the government think it could take over the tottering old Grand Trunk and keep it alive? Did they even think—Heaven forbid!—that they could take over and run the so successful, so complex Canadian Pacific?

After a short stay in Ottawa to study this important facet of his new position, Arthur returned to Toronto to find a house in Toronto for his family. Lizzie would remain for a while in Sudbury near the doctor who was still keeping a close eye on her, and Bertha would stay with her mother for the time being. It happened to be a light winter this year, so they would be able to take a few therapeutic walks together, just to get Lizzie on her feet again.

Zoë, already in Toronto, was prepared to help her father house-hunt. She had moved into the Elm Street "Y," settling into her second term at the Toronto Normal School, preparing for a teaching career. Not her idea of a great future, she told her father. His response was firm: she must stick it out this year so as to have her teacher's certificate, guaranteeing her a respectable career, if she ever needed to work. "Humph!" said Zoë. How could anyone hold such old-fashioned ideas about the opportunities for young women? At the end of this term, she privately decided, she would switch direction and register for courses in stenography and shorthand.

Meantime, she gobbled the house-for-sale advertisements in the Toronto *Mail and Empire*. Friends at Normal School told her that Parkdale was considered less stylish these days than the High Park area. Her father's object was not style but ease of getting to work at his new downtown office. On their first Saturday, the two of them took the tramcar west along King Street and then north along Roncesvalles, getting off at intervals to pace the cross streets running west to Parkside Drive. By mid-afternoon they found a brick house listed for immediate sale on Geoffrey Street, three walkable blocks from Roncesvalles and therefore a twenty-minute tramway commute to Arthur's office near the corner of King and Yonge Streets. In the other direction, the Geoffrey house was half a block from High Park. Arthur felt that those gentle wooded slopes, ponds, and walkways would raise Lizzie's spirits. She could slip over to feed the ducks and enjoy the formal gardens. He made an appointment for a serious longer talk with the owner. Then he and Zoë returned to the Walker Hotel for dinner, feeling proud of themselves.

Next day, Arthur suggested they attend church in the small Parkdale church of St. Mary's, where Zoë had been christened. Again, Zoë had insider information: the larger Church of the Epiphany had a fine choir, "Which will certainly suit Bertha better." They had tacitly decided to buy the house on Geoffrey Street.

When Monday morning came, Arthur was delighted to realize that the window of his new office in the tall Canadian Pacific executive building on Yonge Street offered a fine view to the south toward the Lake Ontario shoreline. In the near distance lay the ongoing construction work around the Union Station. That chaotic site no longer belonged to the Grand Trunk Railway. It was now the property of the new Toronto Terminals Railway Company. Plans for a redesign of the station, drawn up early in 1914, had languished in wartime. Arthur sighed and turned back to his desk. His current concern was not the problems of the Toronto Union Station, but the life of the CPR in Ontario.

Zoë joined her father at the Walker Hotel for dinner, with news of a productive afternoon. She had dropped in at a business school on King Street. A young woman at the reception desk offered a welcoming hand and some heartening words, "I'm Maud McCall, and *I* am the manager." Maud's smile slipped a little as she acknowledged that the disappearance of boys who had gone overseas had opened the management job for her. "The war has done more for women than suffragette marches. The typewriter helps too: women are dextrous at the keyboard."

Zoë had never prided herself on manual dexterity, so she shifted the subject. Were many businesses hiring women as office managers? "Indeed yes! And as court reporters, bookkeepers, filing clerks—whatever jobs the men have left behind." Zoë saw a new world opening. She would become a businesswoman on the day she finished the dreary slog at Normal School.

Lizzie and Bertha, on their last day in Sudbury, went to the town hall, to say goodbye to friends and to each receive from the Canadian Red

Cross Society a pin recognizing "WOMEN'S WAR WORK."

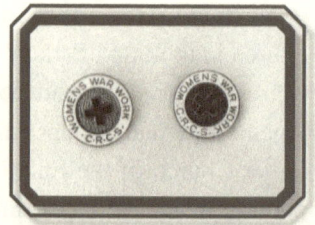

At the end of the week the moving trucks came to Geoffrey Street, and Zoë and her father guessed at the right places for the bigger pieces of furniture, and directed the movers accordingly. Unfortunately, the small living room (nobody would call it a parlour nowadays) was overwhelmed by the dignified Victorian set from Aurora, and the dining room could not squeeze in all six chairs along with the buffet. That extra furniture went into the garage to the rear of the house, empty because the Smiths had no motor car. Upstairs, the master bedroom was at the back of the house, and two small bedrooms at the front. Bertha's bedroom furniture did not quite fit into the first of these, so her dressing table went up to the third-floor space under the eaves. The bedroom set belonging to Zoë sat neatly in the other front room, but she would have to stay on at the "Y" for the next little while, because Lizzie, on Dr. Howey's advice, would occupy this room "for now." Since her attack of angina, Lizzie had become a light and restless sleeper. Arthur profoundly hoped she would recuperate soon. He would miss her gentle presence in the big double bed with its fine carved headboard. The movers left, and Zoë unpacked and placed everything, from the pictures and pillows to the kitchen tools: meat grinders, potato masher, egg beater, nutmeg grater, bean pot, cherry huller, jelly molds.

When Lizzie and Bertha arrived, they showed strong feelings that Arthur and Zoë had erred in selecting a house too small for the family's possessions. Nevertheless, Lizzie found comfort in the new coal furnace in the basement, next to the washing tubs, and Bertha was certainly delighted to be back in Toronto.

No one dared complain about living space when they read the newspaper stories about the winter of 1916 in the trenches overseas: frostbite, insect infestation, mud, and misery. The Canadian Overseas Railway Construction Corps, which so many men who were friends of the Smiths had joined, were building railways through blasted terrain to the front-line area, bringing in stores and ammunition, and carrying casualties to hospitals in the rear.

The three young engineer-soldiers were now in the area near the Somme River in France. Jim Laing wrote from the Front, cheerful as always: *"We are now part of the 3rd Canadian Tunnelling Company. That is a lot better than being trench-diggers, since we know so much about things like working 20 feet underground and using ammonal. We are still in ▇▇▇▇"* (But here the censors had obviously cut some phrases). *"Look it up in your high school atlas.—Your loving Jim."*

No one at home in Toronto knew that at this very moment six teams of soldiers in the Royal Canadian Engineers, each led by a young officer, were burrowing twenty feet beneath the ground near St. Eloi. They were creating subterranean galleries beneath No Man's Land, working from the Canadian line toward the German one with orders to establish a cache of explosives at the end of each tunnel. If this new scheme worked, the tide of the war might turn on the Western Front.

All of that was secret. But by the middle of March, the Toronto *Star* had to tell its readers that things had gone wrong in the distant war zone. Some hint of the tunnelling must have reached German ears. Someone must have talked carelessly, or perhaps German spy rings worked more efficiently than the British could believe. Alerted to the underground threat, the Germans had quietly moved their centres of strength farther north. When the secret caches exploded, the damage they did was largely neutralized.

Of six possible areas of devastation, only two proved effective. The other four simply left huge craters in No Man's Land, without damage to the enemy.

"Jim must be in terrible danger," Bertha cried, shuddering at thought of the tunnelling. But Jim's next letter, breezy as usual, lacked any reference to St. Eloi and the misdirected explosives.

Coincidentally, a letter from Dan Hillman arrived for Bertha, directed "care of A.L. Smith, Esq., CPR, Sudbury, Ontario" and forwarded from there to Toronto. Perhaps no one had told Dan of the Smiths' move. Anyway, Arthur handed it to her, saying how good it was of his old friend to find time to write to her, as well as to send a long letter to himself, explaining as much as possible about action on the Front.

Like Jim, Dan made no mention of the war to Bertha. Rather, he wrote about what he was reading, or, in particular, rereading. Ruskin's *The Stones of Venice* had kindled his interest in Italy when he was in Ridgetown High School, he wrote. *"That was in 1890, when I was twelve, and you, my dear young person, were probably still a babe in arms."*

Bertha rather enjoyed being referred to as a young person. She would celebrate her twenty-sixth birthday in September, and was not feeling particularly young. But she wrote back cheerfully that she had dug out her old college text and reread the excerpts from *The Stones of Venice*. She too loved the long rolling description of the approach to the beautiful city: *"where it magnified itself along the waves, as the quick silent pacing of the gondola drew nearer and nearer."* What an escape from Toronto! She drifted into a dream of travelling. It would be foolish to mention her yearning, given the hardships Dan was enduring, so she swept into a comic resumé of her college "Eng. Lit." classes, slipping back into that carefree time as she wrote.

No answer came from Dan for a while. However, in June, Mary Jaffray forwarded an item from the Sudbury *Star* about local soldiers. It included the fact that Dan had been "mentioned in dispatches" for bravery under fire, and had been promoted "in the field" to the rank of major in summer of 1916. A surprising time for him to be dreaming of gondolas!

That summer, Zoë, having enlivened endless dinner conversations with discussions on the relative value of Pitman versus Gregg as systems of shorthand, the labour situation in Toronto, the difficult rise of the New Woman, and the awful price of a good lunch at a King Street cafe-

teria, gratefully left the teachers' world of blackboards and textbooks, and began her search for a niche in the world of business. Within a week, Maud McCall had a position lined up for her. Just a replacement job, filling in for someone away on sick leave, Maud warned, but it would give practical experience, and hope of a good letter of reference later.

Bertha's life also brightened as she won a soloist's place at the Church of the Epiphany, picked up on part-time study at the old Conservatory of Music, and tried out for a place in the Mendelssohn Choir. She dwelt on all these activities in her weekly notes to Jim. One of his letters to her slipped past the censor with a grumble about old-fashioned military regulations that impeded the tunnellers. An occasional letter still came from Dan also, less personal now and confined to general comments about his work: laying tracks when the army advanced, ripping them up when it retreated, and evacuating casualties to ambulance dressing stations.

The Toronto newspapers filled in the gaps in these letters. The lists of casualties coming from the battles along the Somme River grew ever longer, with deaths in the thousands, wounded in action in the tens of thousands. There was no remission in the battles and of the deathly toll. After the battle of Courcelette, Canadian casualties amounted to 24,629.

At the Christmas season, exciting notes from Jim and Roddy and Ken described their first sighting of Royal Air Force planes flying on reconnaissance duty. How the young tunnellers envied the airmen so far from the trenches! *"Yet we know we are as important as the boys that fly!"* Jim wrote. Cousin Mearle sent other news: Dr. Craig McLaren had gone overseas with the Canadian Army Medical Corps. *"And without marrying Miss Gordon first!—to our surprise!"*

Before the Christmas holidays ended, a more important surprise arrived by wire from Montreal headquarters. The Vice-President of the Canadian Pacific Railway wanted to talk to "A.L. Smith, in person."

Unusual! Senior officers rarely dealt with mid-level personnel. The new Vice-President, Edward Beatty, was senior only in the sense of rank and power. At thirty-eight years of age he was unusually young to have acted already as General Counsel of the huge CPR, and to have become its Vice-President in 1914.

Arthur reserved a berth on the sleeping car for that night, packed a valise, and kept the appointment on the next day, January 3rd. No records remain to tell what happened in that meeting. Arthur's family never knew what kind of conversation ensued, what proffering of possibilities, what assurances of confidentiality, what specification of time limits. The consequences of the interview became clear quickly, however.

On January 31, 1917, A.L. Smith left his position as Superintendent of the Ontario division of the Canadian Pacific, to become General Manager of the Algoma Eastern Railway. The previous holder of that position was an older man, ready to resign. Arthur must have seemed like the best possible replacement. He knew the Algoma line well from his days in Sudbury, and he had an excellent reputation as a good manager in that area. The Board of the Algoma Eastern welcomed him as its new director. Maybe they felt they were stealing a march on the CPR by luring away one of its men.

Undoubtedly, Arthur's surprising agreement to make this move after twenty-six years with the CPR was indirectly related to the Royal Commission's suggestion that the Canadian government take over the bankrupt Grand Trunk Pacific, buy up a number of lesser lines, and launch a new nationally owned company. Obviously, the Canadian Pacific Railway had decided to do some buying of its own in order to forestall the new national railway from gaining dominance. There were rumours, however, that the Algoma Eastern had rejected recent offers of purchase from the CPR. Maybe there was an alternative takeover plan behind the CPR's quiet acceptance of A.L. Smith's surprise departure? Well, if he was involved in a tunnelling manoeuvre on the part of the Canadian Pacific, so be it.

At any rate, Arthur could tell Lizzie confidentially that he would not have to sacrifice his pension or his seniority in the CPR. He could also promise that he would repeat the pattern established when he was in charge of Farnham, Quebec. He would work in Algoma during the week, and spend long weekends with the family. They would not have to move again.

n i n e t e e n

Locomotive
Algoma, 1917

The family, in fact, hardly took notice of his return to the Geoffrey Street house. Bertha was standing in the front hall, the telephone receiver in her hand. "It's Mrs. Laing in Sudbury," she whispered and heavily dropped the receiver. Arthur picked it up to hear Mrs. Laing's cry, "No, no, Bertha! He's alive! It's terrible but it's not that terrible." Arthur heard the distant voice reading from a telegram.

> *This is to inform you that Captain James Laing has been seriously injured in a severe explosion, and will be sent home to Canada by the next available hospital ship.*

Arthur replaced the receiver, and turned to Bertha, hastily agreeing that she should go at once to Sudbury to comfort Mrs. Laing. Lizzie hurried downstairs to hear both sets of news: about Jim, and about Arthur's interview in Montreal.

Bertha left for Sudbury the next day, having wired Mrs. Laing of her coming. Within a fortnight, her father was also on his way north, feeling his way into his new position.

On that first trip, as on the many he would make in the next months between Toronto and Sudbury, Arthur lay awake. The throb of the locomotive working to pull the train of cars through the darkness reawakened his youthful fascination with the way trains worked. He could still visualize the scene in the engine:

the fireman heaving shovelfuls of coal into the open-doored furnace to keep the boiler on the bubble, the dark smoke flying up the escape route of the stack, shooting smoke and sometimes sparks into the darkness above farms and villages; the engineer, hand on the throttle, eyes alert for signals, watching the cluster of gauges as he controlled the flow of steam power piped from boiler to pistons; the pistons themselves, reciprocating as they beat power through to the main wheels. And then through all the couplings and connections, the small wheels turning, so fast the eye could see hardly anything—just a blur, driven by the locomotive power along the ready rails, over the ballast on land and the struts on bridges.

Arthur lay, wakeful, more than ever aware of the obsessive sounds and movements of the night train. Drifting into a waking dream, he internalized the drive of the engine, as he had done in dreams since boyhood. In his adult years he had considered signals and spikes and timetables and junctions. He had almost lost that sense of driving wheels turning and small wheels responding. Maybe many other men who had spent their lives working on the railways had once had the same dream of connecting with mysterious power. He slipped into sleep, touched a memory of a bookplate he had once seen, and dropped into a dream of the mythic Pegasus, accompanying the engine wheels in its flight.

Arthur awoke in the morning, glad to be travelling to Sudbury to start his strange new assignment. He would arrange to rent a comfortable room in the Balmoral hotel at the corner of Elm and Elgin Streets for his recurring stay-overs, and then go a lit-tle farther down Elm to the Algoma Eastern office and begin work on reports, records, decisions, and projections. Soon he would go on to the human side of setting up. He would take the Algoma Eastern train from Sudbury to Espanola and on down to Little Current on Manitoulin Island. He would introduce himself to the staff of the Algoma Eastern Railway at each major junction. Then he would leave them for a week or so—leave them to chew over the changes his coming foreshadowed.

While her father planned these preliminary moves, Bertha heard news of Jim's progress from a nursing station at the Front, to a hospital in England. Until he was brought to Canada, she would wait at home in Toronto through the cold grey winter of 1917, darkened further by the continuing sorry news from Flanders and France.

It was even colder in northern Ontario, but at least it was bright. The snow on either side of the train track sparkled in the winter sun as Arthur rode on his first official trip along the Algoma Eastern Railway to its southernmost point. A local map became clearer in his head as the train moved past the stopping points. Many of them were named for natural resources: Copper Cliff, Macmillan Gold Mine, Lawson Quarry. Others suggested the regional geography: Fox Lake,  Whitefish Falls, Swift Current on Manitoulin Island, Little Current at the end of the AER line. The track twisted around hard rock ridges, crossed swamp areas on platforms of corduroy timber and ballast, and the train pumped through clay hills.

En route, Arthur introduced himself to the staff: the agents at the larger stations and the maintenance men on the permeant way. He also made a quick assessment of the physical equipment: the locomotives, the switches, the rolling stock, the flag stop shelters.

A letter from Dan was waiting for him on his return to Sudbury—a surprisingly grim one. *"It seemed bad enough to follow advancing troops but when they retreat all common sense seems to depart and right in the middle Col. Ramsey was recalled and I was appointed RCE5 and promoted to Lt. Col. I was a whole week without going to bed."* In plain terms, Dan had moved into command via promotion on the field. Perhaps because he was now the commanding officer, he had also played the role of censor, cutting out personal details of his current life.

Once again, there was a note to be forwarded to Bertha. Here too there was no talk of reading or music. Even the handwriting seemed different, as though he had simply copied a report sent off to his superiors: *"During the Cambrai battle we had trouble getting rail service up to the new front, but were able to prefabricate a timber bridge across the canal."* How to answer such a grim letter?

She told him how vivid she always found his description of life at the Front, even when he was obviously conforming to censorship rules. She wrote, *"You do sound desperately tired. Will you be given leave? Could you possibly get a chance to go to Italy?"* After this there was a hiatus in his letters.

Her sense of living in suspended time grew stronger. The hospital in England did not release Jim until the superficial burns were healed and some of the metal debris was removed from his chest and arms. It  was late in February before the hospital ship arrived in convoy at Halifax, another week before a train brought a carload of wounded men into the Toronto station, and yet another three weeks before the families were assured that the wounded soldiers were sufficiently settled at the Spadina Military Hospital to receive visitors. Jim's mother went with her daughters and Bertha for the initial visit at the Toronto "hospital"—a quickly converted Knox College. The nursing sisters only allowed visits by one person at a time. Mrs. Laing, who went first, came back in tears. "My boy, in this frightening place, and I couldn't kiss him for fear of infection. Well, Bertha, it's your turn."

Jim's face, thin to the point of looking skeletal, was strangely crisscrossed with healing scars, but being Jim, he was trying to smile. Bertha slipped into the chair by his bed. "Oh Jim, don't try to talk to me." The half-smile faded as Jim raised both hands in a curious pushing-away gesture. The nurse's quiet voice explained. "We think it indicates a dream of the collapsing tunnel." A dream? Was he asleep? The nurse nodded. The visit was over.

If Bertha felt suspended in time in the first months of 1917, Zoë felt the reverse. Things were happening almost fast enough for her. In the offices of the provincial government, the Secretary of the Head of the Bureau of Labour and Trades announced that he was going to enlist. The Under-Secretary was promoted to fill his job. A new Under-Secretary was needed to look after the real work of the Department. Maud McCall slotted Zoë in for an interview. "Aim to make a good impression," Maud advised. "But don't appear too good."

Zoë, following this devious advice, danced carefully through her job interview. In her joy at hearing the job was hers, Zoë bought herself a "tailor-made lady's suit" in the new rather masculine fashion, featuring a skirt rather shorter than Lizzie considered proper. But to the group of men and women that Zoë was now happily working with, it seemed appropriate.

Arthur, quietly easing into his new life, found some of the same happiness. He had established a comfortable routine: short work weeks in the north, long weekends with his family in Toronto. It was a separation like the one they had experienced while he worked at Farnham.

Through his connection with Harry McLean, he arranged a speedup in the construction of a pair of important spurs connecting the Algoma Eastern to two of the new mining endeavours still springing up in the area. He managed the transfer of two locomotives from the CPR to the AER yards—two rather old-fashioned "Baldwins." Arthur smiled at the familiar name, but this company was in no way related to the Aurora Mills. The locomotives, though not the latest in design, were considerably better than the engines the AER had been using.

Jack Hammell, taking a break from his promotional tour out west, jollied Arthur into joining him in a business-related jaunt along the Algoma Eastern. Jack peered with interest at the spur lines leading off the main track to the Mond Mines, International Nickel, and other growing enterprises. Arthur was more intrigued by the sight of a preliminary clearing for a proposed new spur. For him, this spearhead into dense forest stirred dreams of possible construction and profitable usage.

At Espanola they transferred to the CPR line running west to Sault Ste. Marie. There they spent some time poking round the old Sault enterprises. Smelters, foundries, paper and steel mills, shipping sheds, all were the legacy of an early visionary entrepreneur named Francis Clergue. Jack  Hammell, an equally enterprising man in his own mining world, restlessly urged Arthur to move on. He proposed that they take a trip north of "the Soo," on the Algoma Central Railway (another of Clergue's projects) as far as the spur leading into the Agawa Canyon. This line was reputed to offer a breathtaking trip over high trestles and under overhanging crags.

They left the small CPR station and crossed over to the much grander Algoma Central and Hudson Bay Railway station. This solid edifice marked the eminence of the city's numerous railway and steamship lines. They were told, however, that the popular side trip had unfortunately been suspended until spring. Their foray into the famous canyon would have to be put off until some other time.

They travelled back on the CPR branch line to Espanola and then further east on the AER. Jack speculated about the future of this ore-rich, half-empty terrain, while Arthur eased back into the more humdrum thoughts of a man managing a modest local railway. In Sudbury the two friends parted company.

Arthur walked over to the CPR station to pick up Bertha, who was just arriving from Toronto for a first visit to Jim Laing in his new setting. Sudbury's best hospital, l'Hopital Saint-Joseph, a Catholic organization, had originally refused to shift into war services and accept Jim as a patient. Eola, Jim's friend since high school days, heard this with fury and paid a high-pitched visit to Sister Marie-Ephron, the administrative officer. Eola convinced her that a Sudbury boy-hero deserved special care, and Jim had now been transferred from the Spadina Hospital to Sudbury.

Sister Marie-Ephron welcomed Bertha. But with a warning: there was no prognosis as to Jim's general recovery, and no guess about whether he would ever return to work as a mining engineer. The visit itself told her nothing more. Jim was still locked into a frightening silence, unbroken by her presence. She returned the next day, accompanied by Mab Moore. She hoped Mab's voice, linked with happier times, might lift Jim into response. His only reaction was a lifting of his hands again, as if pushing away a pressure.

When spring turned into summer, Arthur travelled again to Sault Ste. Marie. It was time for the semi-annual meeting of the Board of the Lake Superior Corporation, the company that had hired him in January as General Manager of their railway. Three elderly businessmen quizzed him quietly about his work and his view of the future, said a courteous thanks, and concluded the meeting.

Arthur decided to seize the opportunity to enjoy the trip once planned with Jack Hammell. He travelled north by himself from the Sault to the Agawa Canyon. Once on board, his boyhood sense of the romance of  railroading revived. He imagined the sheer audacity of the engineers who had envisioned this high suspension line, the workers who lifted the giant girders into space, the first engine drivers who dared to pull a train along  the bridge slung miles above the canyon floor. The shrill train whistle, blowing back to the passenger cars across the chasm, seemed unearthly, as if it sounded a human defiance to the norms of nature. Arthur felt an intensified sense of being in an unreal position in this wilderness world, like the soldiers lifted out of all norms by the malignity of war.

No private word had come from Vice-President Beatty about how long his northern tenure would last. Presumably there were machinations beneath the visible surface of things. Yet Arthur had begun to count the days nervously in eagerness to get back to the Ontario Division, as the pistons of war powered on.

twenty

Ballast
World War, 1917–18

From a campsite near the battleground, Dan wrote Bertha to thank her for sympathizing when he groused about life at the Front. *"Your letters act as ballast for me. We engineers can only build a good line of track on a strong bed of small stones—ballast. Unfortunately, all our train rides in Belgium are jarring, since there are no small ballasting stones left here. But your letters let me ride smoothly in imagination—to Italy, or back home to Canada."* Ballast—Bertha thought that was also an appropriate metaphor for Dan's letters to her. They steadied her.

She wrote to him with her own news: she had joined the Mendelssohn Choir in performance at Massey Hall. At home, she had taken over management of the housework, in order to shield her mother from recurring attacks of angina. She found this responsibility another kind of ballast in the dark days of November. She did not know whether she should mention that his friend Harry McLean had forwarded a copy of the official announcement that Dan had once again been "mentioned in a Despatch." The announcement was signed by Winston Churchill, the young Secretary of State for War.

It was easier to decide not to mention to Dan her regular, worrisome visits to the Sudbury Hospital. Jim, his wounds nearly healed, still lingered there, his halting talk stirred now by fragmentary memories of Vimy Ridge. Bertha wondered if he even remembered all those happy summer visits when he had laughed about becoming engaged to her. The new Jim could not laugh; he could barely smile at his visitors.

Jim was not the only soldier who had been sent home from the war. Near the end of 1917, Arthur's brother Harry Batoche Smith, seriously wounded in the Somme battles, was invalided out of the army, and brought back to Canada on a hospital ship. Arthur joined his parents at Union Station to see Harry in the interval between trains. After waiting in a frantic crowd, they glimpsed him, accompanied by a nurse. He had lost his hearing during severe shelling, she explained. The family tried without success to engage with him before the conductor cried "All aboard!" and the train for Edmonton pulled out. Arthur was left with sadness for his younger brother, but also with guilt about his parents. He had not visited them once during this peripatetic year.

His spirits were low enough without this plunge. Vice-President Beatty showed no signs of ending his northern exile. Maybe Mr. Beatty was too absorbed in greater concerns to care about the Algoma district. First, the American government had taken over wartime control of all railway services in the USA to back up the new movement of American soldiers, and the Canadian Pacific faced a possibility that the US might claim a right to control CPR lines within the American borders. At the same time, the new National Defence Board of Canada was forcing the CPR to cut the number of passenger trains this year, to conserve fuel and facilitate movement of freight materials. Both governments were obviously exerting enough new pressures to distract the CPR vice-president from any interest in the little Algoma railway. Arthur, as its general manager, must continue his here-again, gone-again life for the foreseeable future.

His family had become indifferent to this routine. Lizzie had developed a habit of taking quiet walks down Geoffrey Street to Parkside Road and into High Park. Even though winter was now closing in, she managed to maintain these healthy and soul-satisfying walks. They eased a little of the guilt she felt about shifting her domestic responsibilities to Bertha.

On her next visit to Sudbury, Bertha found some relief from her other burden, the continuing anxiety about Jim. Eola Hammell, in town for a brief visit with her parents, accompanied her and Mab Moore to the hospital. Together they read Jim the latest letters from Roddy and Ken, who were "still tunnelling" but missing Jim's company. Jim listened, apparently unmoved. Eola found his lassitude very upsetting. Jack must come and see him soon, she said. Maybe it was not memories of war that wounded him still, but lack of hope for the future he had trained for. She would speak to Jack about it.

Zoë struck one happy note as 1917 ended. She was promoted to the position of Assistant to the Minister of Labour in the Ontario government. "I should really have the title of Under-Secretary," she explained. She would have the title as well as the job, once she had put in enough time in the office to qualify. "And guess what? My boss, Mr. Riddell, is a fan of Professor Leacock! He's delighted to have someone in the Department of Labour who studied Economics!" Neither Lizzie nor Bertha found this totally exciting.

Next day Zoë came home with another surprise. She had been to a hairdresser and had her hair "bobbed." She advised Bertha to follow suit. "I couldn't!" Bertha protested. The closest to an erotic fantasy she had ever permitted herself was a dream of a moment when someone would pull the hairpins gently out of her dark hair and release its gentle fall. Zoë's mother was more blunt: "You look scalped." But Zoë had simmered down already; she had more important news than the bobbing of her hair. Mr. Riddell had spoken with praise about a bit of research she had done on international labour regulations.

Arthur, when told this part of Zoë's news next weekend, privately thought that Zoë had inherited her problem-solving ability from him. He felt abashed as he realized how little time he had spent talking to her about the work of the Ministry of Labour. Surely with all his experience in labour conditions, labour codes—and labour troubles too— he could have helped her expand on the facts she had been researching and feeding to her new employer. His spells of work at the Algoma Eastern offices in Sudbury had turned him into a part-time participant in family affairs.

From overseas, Dan wrote to Bertha that he too had found a time of lighter responsibility. He had been granted a short leave after the Battle of Passchendaele in November, and wangled a train trip to Italy. *"I have sent you a little mosaic picture of doves, made from the stones of Venice. The first time I heard you sing, it was about longing to fly away on 'The Wings of a Dove.' These doves are not flying away—they are together, balancing on the edge of a golden bowl."*

Unfortunately, there was no parcel accompanying the letter. Bertha wrote back quickly, however, expressing delight about his visit to the place he had dreamed about, and telling him she was eager to see the gift he had sent. "It will arrive some day for sure, just as your letter has done."

By Christmas, no parcel had appeared. But Arthur received a package from overseas, containing a picture of the current officers of the Canadian Overseas Railway Construction Corps: Dan sat at the left in the front row. His former commanding officer, Colin Ramsey, stood in the middle at the back. Sadly, these six men were the only survivors of the twenty-six officers who had posed so cheerfully in Longmoor Camp in 1915, before their embarkation.

Spring of 1918 brought more dramatic news. The Toronto papers announced that Dan had been named to the Distinguished Service Order. The DSO was regarded with some of the awe attributed to winners of the Victoria Cross, which was awarded to "men in the ranks," soldiers or sailors, not officers, who committed single acts of outstanding bravery. The Distinguished Service Order was instead awarded only "to an Officer in the field, for consistent leadership and extraordinary valour." At the same time, Colonel Ramsey was awarded the Order of St. Michael and St. George (OMG) for his role in creating and leading the Corps. He and Dan were given transport to England together to receive their awards from King George V at Buckingham Palace.

For Arthur Smith, news of all this drama of railroading overseas threw into sharp contrast his undramatic life on the sleepy northern frontier. A more general shadow was cast by knowledge that the Canadian government, charged with settling the fate of the Grand Trunk and the Canadian Northern Railways, both now bankrupt, was now actually considering the creation of a new national line, based on their failed networks. Such a line would offer new competition to the Canadian Pacific

Railway: more trouble for the great company that stretched beyond his little world.

Arthur faced a critical decision. Thanks to his management, the Algoma Eastern Railway was now modernized. It blended with the Canadian Pacific transcontinental enterprise in its construction material, engines, and other running stock. Arthur had done all he could do to permit the CPR to absorb this marginal company into its main line, and to forestall a Grand Trunk takeover. Was that not enough? He had completed a year and a half in what had been presented to him as a brief cloak-and-dagger exercise, but which now felt like unending exile.

As he rode the Canadian Pacific Company's trains back and forth every other week, no longer sleeping away the miles in a comfortable berth but sitting in the parlour car, smoking a pipe and pondering, he determined to change his pattern of existence. So much was happening in this summer of 1918, especially in the world of railways. He would move beyond the little paths in Algoma.

In July, when Bertha accompanied him to Sudbury on one of these trips, a change loomed in her life also. Sister Marie-Ephron greeted her with news. "Monsieur 'Ammell has been to see Capitaine Jim. We have a miracle!" Sister said.

Jack Hammell, on a fly-in visit from Flin Flon, had bypassed general chat and cut directly to an offer. As soon as the medicos said it was safe, Jim could go to work for him. Not in an underground mine, but as a technical assistant who would advise on all of Jack's contemplated mining projects. Jack told him gruffly that he himself had come a long way without any education in geology, but that at this crucial moment in his career he needed help from someone with "formal know-how." He ordered Jim to mull over what he was offering: not a kindly stop-gap for a weary warrior, but a job, a good job that would challenge him as a graduate mining engineer.

Tough-speaking Jack had done what soft-voiced sympathizers could not do; he had set Jim on the way to mental and moral recovery, to match his physical progress. A miracle, as Sister Marie-Ephron said. But when Bertha entered the ward she found no sign of change in Jim's response to her, no sense of anything special about her visits.

Arthur, on the other hand, had now reconstituted himself as a special visitor in Toronto railway stations. Whenever he was back from Sudbury, he began dropping in to chat with some of his old colleagues at Parkside, Leaside, North York, and elsewhere. He found dispatchers and station masters nearly overwhelmed by sudden shifts in traffic as wartime movement reached a climax. Many of these railwaymen, whether old acquaintances or newcomers, welcomed the relief of having "A.L." offer to help with swift adjustments in schedules.

Everywhere he heard of a fierce sense of urgency in forwarding materials to back up the last great attack in Europe. There was also a sharp increase in scheduling problems, as more hospital trains asked permission to expedite their passage from Saint John, Quebec City, or Montreal. Greater loads of wounded men needed swifter trips to home hospitals. A.L. Smith became quietly involved in expediting the wartime movement in and through Toronto—and no one seemed to mind. Perhaps no one in the higher echelons even noticed.

That suspicion was ratified in October, 1918. A new regime emerged without public preamble at CPR headquarters. President Thomas Shaughnessy reached sixty-five and retired as president. To the surprise of many old-timers, his place was filled by Edward Beatty. At forty-two years old, he was much the youngest man ever to hold such a crucial position. He was also the first Canadian-born president of the Company. The negotiations that preceded this advance, as well as the rising tensions of the war, must have preoccupied Beatty over the past year, Arthur told himself. He found comfort in this supposition.

As the new regime began in the Company's headquarters, Arthur allowed himself to drift into devoting more and more of his time to reviving connections in Toronto. His perspective and intentions were changing. Recent experiences in the north had led him into moments of unusual introspection. Time had slowed down for him. Toronto helped him climb back into a brisker mode. The analytical, practical control that had steadied him throughout his adult life was restored. He could now stifle any sense of being bypassed by events, and rejoin the life of swift action and practical decisions that had characterized his earlier career.

In November, rumours about an end to the war gave way to facts, news stories, meetings in Ottawa, and excitement in Bay Street. The long-awaited final push in Europe seemed to be happening. From overseas, Dan wrote to Arthur that he had been instructed to gather all the information he could about the railways, which would be needed in Europe to cope with the withdrawal of troops after an armistice. He flew over the possible routes on November 9th with a fighter escort. His corps had orders to prepare to manage the evacuation of the fighting forces and also to facilitate the advance of occupying troops moving into the reclaimed zone.

Then came the truly significant news: the warring, exhausted nations had agreed to an armistice on November 11. Exuberant crowds streamed down Yonge Street in an impromptu parade. Zoë and Jessie Laing and Maud McCall joined the crowd. Late in the afternoon they took a streetcar back to the west end, exhausted but jubilant, though all too ready to break into tears. Ironically, the evening newspaper listed the soldiers who were killed on the very day that peace was signed.

Arthur had to wait until the jubilation died down to see if the armistice brought a change in his own position. His hopes were buoyed by an auspicious encounter just before Christmas. As he got off the train from Toronto onto the Sudbury platform, the transcontinental from the west pulled in on the opposite track and a group of men stepped down, presumably to stretch their legs during the train stop. Someone suddenly called across the tracks, "A.L.!" and waved. Arthur happily called back "D.C.!" to Mr. Coleman, now the Senior Vice-President of the CPR. Years ago, this man had given him friendly advice about moving from London to Montreal. Now he was shouting, "Great to see you!" The Vice-President's secretary cleared his throat; his boss must get back onto the train for Montreal. A final smile and a wave, a screech of air as the brakes released, and the train began to roll away. Arthur's smile remained. It was good to be assured that someone in the upper echelons remembered and valued him.

twenty-one

Brakes
Parkside, 1918–1919

For most of Toronto, the final days of 1918 were euphoric. The war was over. The novelties of war—airplanes, motorcycles, electrification—became commonplace. But not everyone had come home: fallen warriors, known and unknown, were buried somewhere in Europe, and living rebuilders like Dan stayed on. The High Command in Britain decreed that the Canadian Overseas Railway Construction Corps must remain in France to rebuild the north European track system.

Though he presented an appearance of briskness, control, and hopefulness before his troops, Dan felt frustration and dejection. He swung into a happier mood as he wrote Bertha that he was glad to hear her news: she was singing in public again as a soprano soloist, as she should be. A month after the armistice was signed, choirs from several Toronto churches prepared to present *The Messiah* in the Church of the Epiphany. On that December evening, Bertha's first solo rang out in full force: *"Rejoice! Rejoice! Rejoice greatly!"* What a cry! The armistice brought little rejoicing to an audience still assessing the personal and social damage wrought by the war. So, as the cantata unfolded, Bertha sang for them again, releasing a prayer in a voice so gentle this time that it was almost a whisper, *"Peace, . . . Peace."*

Peace was a difficult concept for her. Others could look forward to a quick return of men from overseas. Though Jim Laing was home already, in a sense he still seemed to linger hopelessly in the bombed-out tunnel near Artois. As for Dan, the time for his return to England to be decommissioned was still uncertain. She might have to wait a year before their relationship shifted from correspondence into face-to-face encounters. She had never told Dan about her unresolved engagement to Jim Laing, although it was hard to believe that gossip about it had never seeped through in overseas mail.

Dan's letters took on a more intense tone as the weeks went by. He wrote at greater length of his increasingly fierce desire to return from rebuilding war-damaged railways to take his place in Canada's new world of peace. The photograph he sent her father at Christmas showed him looking tired, sadder, and older than the dark-haired man she remembered. When Bertha wrote in a lighter tone about Zoë's progress in the postwar Department of Labour at Queen's Park in Toronto, Dan offered no comment on Zoë's news, other than to ask, "So what is Miss Bertha doing while her sister runs the Department of Labour?" The answer to that question was still "Not very much."

Arthur could have given the same answer. His life was at a standstill. A month and a half since the Armistice of November 11, 1918, the new happiness of a peaceful Christmas season revived his expectation. Surely now, for sure, someone would let him go back to "normal life," that is, to a real job in the great company that had been his background, his ideal, his pride for thirty-three years. But no word came.

As 1919 began, he could only hope that his current work was still significant in a time of major transition in the railway world. E.J. Chamberlin, Hays' successor as head of the Grand Trunk, had lost his battle against the new Canadian Prime Minister Robert Borden. Backed by a Royal Commission, Borden announced that given the long-time public funding of the GTR, the "rightful owners" of the Grand Trunk Railway were the Canadian people. In February, 1919, Borden, hoping to salvage what he could from the bankruptcy of the Grand Trunk, the Grand Trunk Pacific, and the Canadian Northern Railways, suggested they might be consolidated into a new Canadian transcontinental railway, to become the property of the nation.

This publicly owned railway would of course carry on the old competition against the privately-owned Canadian Pacific. In the Lake Superior region, thanks to President Beatty's strategy and Arthur's dogged holding action, the new national railway could not claim the Algoma Eastern among the companies swept up as part of their conglomerate. But here was A.L. Smith, still in the role of manager of a no-account little railway, while the mighty CPR shook itself out of its wartime troubles and got to work on its main lines.

Over the past two years Arthur's family had adjusted to his biweekly trips to Sudbury. In turn, he had hardly been aware that Lizzie was also venturing into small repetitive travels. Conscripting Bertha as a travelling companion, she had ben paying biweekly visits to her father in Aurora. Bertha's reward for the unexciting trips was a renewed friendship with Grandpa Baldwin's caregiver, her cousin Gertrude Baldwin. Gertrude, like Eola Jaffray, had been a long-ago playmate of Bertha's.

Bertha travelled alone when she paid her monthly visit to Jim in Sudbury. Jim was talking now, a little more easily, about tunnelling and Courcelette and other battles of the Somme. But he never mentioned the sunny day on McGregor Bay when he had proposed to her and she had nodded assent. Her visits left her in a sense of abeyance, similar (though she was unaware of it) to her father's present state.

Her feeling of pique was mollified when the long-awaited parcel from Dan arrived after a very long detour. Addressed to "A.L. Smith, Sudbury," the present from Venice had travelled first to the well-known town of Sudbury in England. There the postmaster wasted considerable time hunting up all the Smiths in the Suffolk neighbourhood without locating an "A.L." Eventually, someone noticed that the return address was that of an officer in the Canadian army, and took a chance on forwarding it to Sudbury, Ontario. Slowly, by ocean voyage and train, it reached the post office in Canada's Sudbury. There it languished again, before eventually slipping along to Toronto. Lizzie and her daughters watched Arthur unwrap layer after layer, until the gift emerged, handsomely framed, a beautiful little picture. It was formed of hundreds of tiny pieces of marble, in every shade of white, beige, grey, and amber, set against a black background. Venetian artists had cut the marble into shapes, and set them, softly shading together to create a picture of doves, perched on the rim of a golden bowl.

Arthur was delighted to receive such a charming gift. He still considered Dan to be primarily his own friend. Many of Dan's letters to Arthur had included technical details about construction problems overseas, such as, *"The Germans blasted every second joint of the rails and exploded a mine every 100 meters, blasted all water facilities, etc."* In other letters to his older friend, Dan had shared distressing references to postwar scenes of general devastation: *"To think that people, Germans as well as French and Belgians could build so powerfully, and then turn to destruction. Churches, town halls, homes, stores, sad enough, but somehow the remains of a bombed-out forest or a blasted garden or park seem worse."*

Arthur had passed along some of Dan's notes—even the troubled ones—to Bertha, but he had remained blithely unaware of the increasing intensity of the correspondence between his daughter and his friend. Now, presuming that the much-travelled Venetian treasure was his, Arthur placed it carefully on the mantelpiece, so that all the family could see and enjoy it. Zoë looked at it there and secretly thought of happy days when the young men at McGill had fluttered around her and her friends before flying away to the war. But Bertha knew what the gift meant to Dan and herself. The tiny stones fused into a ballast of song and of peace.

Within a few days Arthur received a letter definitely addressed to him, bringing an even more welcome gift. The private secretary of the new President of the Canadian Pacific Railway wrote to advise that A.L. Smith's name had recently been placed before the Board of the Toronto Terminals Railway Company as a candidate for employment as the company's next Superintendent. President Edward Beatty, who was also Chairman of the Board of the Company, now had the pleasure of informing Mr. Smith that the appointment had gone through, effective May 1, 1919. This would not be officially announced for a fortnight, giving Mr. Smith time to confirm his acceptance of it.

Arthur's heart did somersaults. To become Superintendent of the Toronto terminal, during the coming years when the new Union Station would finally move into urgent postwar construction! He calmed down enough to think carefully about the news. The letter did not mention his current position at the Algoma Eastern Railway. President Beatty must know that the old, intransigent Board of Management of the AER still refused to agree to sell their property to him. Yet he must feel assured that a takeover by the Grand Trunk was no longer a danger. Obviously, he had no intention of revealing his personal involvement in Algoma now, any more than during the cryptic meeting two years ago.

Never mind! Until May the first, Arthur was essentially free to wind down his Algoma projects, while quietly developing more connections with Toronto railwaymen. Then he would move into management of the Union Station that was the centre of the Toronto Terminals Company, and would be the jewel of the modern city. He would ease out of his present job like a good engine driver, quietly applying the brakes as he came to a slow stop.

He thought of that metaphor again as he travelled through the icy weather to Sudbury. He remembered from his first days in Aurora what a fuss was made when the old trains came to a stop. As the engineer slowed the locomotive down, brakemen would run along the top of the train, car after car, and turn a control wheel to apply brakes, repeating this mechanical work on each following car until the whole train came to a somewhat bumpy, sometimes jarring and irregular halt. Arthur remembered how often old problems with braking had led to the wrecks that bedevilled him.

A new braking system, invented in 1872 by George Westinghouse, had been accepted almost universally by the time Arthur moved from telegraphy into a wider range of work. By 1912, Westinghouse's improved air brakes used the pressure of air moving through a triple valve to force a brake shoe against each of the wheels on the train, stopping their motion. The whole train could now be stopped

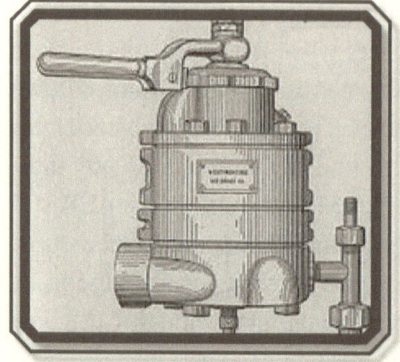
by a single application of the handle on the "triple-drive air brake system" in the engine driver's cab. The engine driver's pressure on the handle would start a movement of air, downward through a triple valve toward the wheels on the engine, and also backward along a brake pipe to the train cars.

As he rode the rails from Toronto, Arthur thanked Westinghouse in his heart for the controlled slowdown at a succession of stations, easing into a final ending, a full stop. That was the way he would withdraw from the Algoma Eastern. He would continue going up and down the line until all his current projects were left neatly complete. Then he would go one last time down the twisting old track, coming to a quiet stop at one small station after another for a series of polite goodbyes.

In this postwar year of 1919, there were rumours of another major change in braking, to be in place possibly in the 1920s. Trains would go beyond the Westinghouse air brakes to an electrical pneumatic system. Without the risks of insufficient air pressure and uneven brake applications, trains would come to a quicker, smooth, and virtually noiseless stop. By then, Arthur thought, he would be in place at the Union Station, and he could participate in experiments with the new system.

Meanwhile, he maintained his two-year-old routine: short working weeks based in Sudbury, long weekends at home with the family. Only Lizzie knew about the major change impending in his work life.

Bertha accompanied him in mid-April, going for her monthly visit to Jim. As usual, she had braced herself for this encounter, though Eola had written to report that Jim was now talking rationally, mostly about Jack's offer of work in the mining world, to begin after his discharge from the hospital. To Bertha's surprise, Jim was waiting in the ambulatory ward, visibly stronger physically than last month. For the first time he thanked her for all her faithful visits. Then came another, major surprise. He mentioned, without preamble, that his mother assumed that he and Bertha must spend all those visits discussing their long-ago talk of marrying. He confessed that he had little memory of those days. "So we must talk about them now."

The talk was not simple. Jim began with a conclusion: "The main thing we had in common, Buffy, was skating." When she added, "And canoeing," Jim diverged into talk of the canoeing he would do with Jack Hammell if the job dream came true. Then he veered back to memories of that summer four years ago. The happiest time, he said, was when Ken and Rod and their girls "got married."

Bertha cut in bluntly. "Jim, do you think that those marriages made you think about you and me getting married too?" His answer was oblique. It was hard for engineers to understand about music and books and flowers and all that, he said. "But Mab and Alice are engineers themselves."

Bertha worked out the base of what he was suggesting: "Maybe you and I were silly to talk about marrying each other?" Jim tried to smile in reply. Afraid to admit how close they both were to tears, they settled for laughter—about the youthful silliness of his "proposal," and the equally silly way she had given him nothing but a nod in answer.

She nodded again now, and laughed, and the fragile web of their "engagement" floated away. Something had come to an end in her life, but the end had come so gently that she hardly sensed the stopping. She left the hospital knowing she would come back, not as the "fiancée" but as a long-time friend and admirer of sturdy, sensible Jim.

Lizzie, taking an afternoon walk along Parkside Drive, listened happily to Bertha's report on the change. How pleasant that this coincided with Arthur's delight in reassuming his place in the Canadian Pacific hierarchy, as Superintendent of the Union Station (though she wished the station site was not so messy looking). And Zoë was doing so well in her office in the Queen's Park government building. Lizzie walked more quickly. Suddenly she felt a tightening in her chest. A pain; a panic: her old warning signal, angina. Bertha scrambled to find the vial of nitroglycerine pills in her mother's purse, and helped her drop onto a park bench. When the pain eased, they crossed the street and slowly walked the half a block to home.

A phone call to her new doctor, an old friend of dear Dr. Howey, brought him on a quick house call. Dr. Perry's presence was calming, and his advice repeated what Dr. Howey would have said: bedrest was essential if Lizzie hoped to escape a heart attack. Dr. Perry talked soothingly about medical advances in the scientific understanding of angina. Sir William Osler had written a fine book called *Angina Pectoris and Allied States*, Dr. Perry said; an old book, but still considered the major text on chest pain and blood pressure. The doctor's voice was so soothing and his presence so reassuring that Lizzie drifted off into sleep.

When she woke, the doctor had left, but Arthur and Zoë had joined Bertha by Lizzie's side. On the doctor's advice, they helped her to bed in the front room. Zoë willingly moved her belongings again, up to the third floor. Bedrest was clearly what Lizzie needed, though she objected to such inactivity.

On May 5th, Arthur was officially appointed Superintendent of the Toronto Terminals Company. Lizzie was still not considered well enough to accompany him to the formal opening of his office in the Union Station, still in the throes of construction.

twenty-two

Ties
Union Station, 1919

On May 24, 1919, the newly installed Superintendent A.L. Smith strode confidently through the western side doors into the Union Station. He  took a quick look to his left at the scaffolding that rose above the spacious concourse of the still unfinished building. Then he moved through the space being temporarily used as a Departures room, with handsome baggage desks and information kiosks, and continued through to the Arrivals room, glorying in the modern benches lined up, neatly in place and ready for the incoming passengers who would someday wait here for connections.

Finally, from the far end of the room, he stepped out onto a temporary wooden bridge in the open air, that led from the "new"—the unfinished—station to the old actual platforms. Moving down a stairway  to the first platform, Superintendent Smith pushed through a crowd of passengers hurrying to and from the tracks. This was the true Departures and Arrivals area.

Today was a holiday, but not for the station people. Conductors checked tickets at the entrance of each platform; dark-skinned porters guarded the steps leading into parlour cars and Pullman sleeping cars of outgoing trains; baggagemen heaved suitcases and trunks onto their wagons and pushed back toward the bridge, bypassed by redcaps carrying valises toward the exits.

Beneath the bridge and behind the station, the trains came and departed in relatively calm order. Many still bore the names of old companies that had been taken over by the federal government this year: the Halifax and Saint John, the Prince Edward Island Railway, and the old Intercolonial, amalgamated now with Mackenzie and Mann's Canadian Northern and the Grand Trunk Pacific. All were now consolidated into a new business organization, On May 21, 1920, the public had learned of another step toward new troubles, new rivalries, facing the CPR. The Canadian government had appointed a Board of Management for a new amalgam of the od lines, titled this year, by order of the Canadian Privy Council, "The new national Canadian railway." Whatever the names, old and new, the passenger trains running east, west, north, and south must all move smoothly through the tangle of tracks lying between the unfinished station and the waterfront of Lake Ontario. As Superintendent of the terminal, A.L. Smith made new and touchy decisions daily about priorities between the old companies that ran along those tracks.

Soon, however, he would entice the Canadian Pacific Company into directing its transcontinental traffic also into and through this tangle of tracks. Since 1906, the CPR had technically been an equal owner of the so-called Union Station, sharing formal ownership with the old Grand Trunk. Yet during the war, the CPR had built a handsome new North Toronto station to be used as its central transfer point. Now the war was over. The CPR's passenger trains should run through the new Union Station, the more central lakeshore facility. That would certainly increase scheduling problems. Nevertheless, in the 1920s the Superintendent of the Central Toronto Terminals would be charged with easing in a postwar phase of railway history. The formal establishment of a second transcontinental Canadian railway would be settled soon, and the two major lines would have to learn to cooperate within Arthur's domain.

But now, as he peered down at the actual lines of track, Arthur recognized a more immediate and urgent problem. Almost all these tracks lay on old crossties. Although modern ties, treated with coal-tar creosote under pressure, had a life span of forty to seventy years, many of the old ties he was looking down at now were untreated and  had probably been set in place as long ago as the 1870s. Visible cracks in the wood of many of them indicated rot. He would have to ask the maintenance director to set up a crew for replacing these old ties as quickly as possible.

His friend Dan, still in Belgium on reconstruction duty, had written about solving a crosstie problem there: *"The only usable wood is in beams in the deserted houses, bars from empty inns and taverns. We even use altar rails from bombed-out churches."* Well—Toronto Union Station would not be reduced to using altar rails to replace its old crossties. Vast forest tracts still waited in the north to be harvested, trees to be sawed into strong eight-foot lengths, logs to be treated with preservatives and used to replace the shabby old ties, both here and in the freight yards closer to the lake.

At the end of the busy day, Arthur walked back through the station for another glimpse of the great potential concourse, then moved happily out of the western Front Street entrance and up to King Street to begin the tram-ride home.

Here was Lizzie, stronger every day. Indeed, she was well enough to take an interest in the garden behind the Geoffrey Street house. She drifted into May dreams of summer colour to come. She had outlasted her bedrest period, though Dr. Perry still advised her to lie down in the afternoon while someone read to her or chatted quietly.

Bertha was the obvious someone. She rescheduled her sessions with the voice coach and reorganized the timing of piano classes with her young pupils and settled quietly—and quite happily—into sharing the joy of reading old favourites and new discoveries with her mother. In private, Bertha read with increasing intensity the expanding flow of letters from Dan, filled now with anticipation of return from his postwar work overseas. She struggled vainly to find a way to tell him about the freedom she now felt, since clearing up her problematic relationship with Jim Laing. She also worried that her father still regarded Dan's friendship with himself as the primary link with the family. The summer months passed vey slowly for her.

In Zoë's world, events moved much more dramatically. The Peace of Versailles evolved, and Canadian diplomats huddled with their international fellows in Switzerland as the new League of Nations emerged. The Ontario government, asked to play a part in establishing an International Labour Office, deputed Zoë's boss, the Honourable Walter Riddell, to set up a Canadian Advisory Commission on International Labour Legislation. Mr. Riddell set Zoë to collect statistics on current international laws designed to protect labour unions and workers' rights, and to guide employers in future labour relations. "Crucially important work!" Zoë announced.

Her father concurred. He remembered the agonizing days of the 1908 railway strike in Montreal. Maybe the end of the war would bring an end to that kind of strife too, he thought. This proved to be a vain hope. A few days after the peaceful celebration of Empire Day, news came from the west about a general strike in Winnipeg. The Toronto *Mail and Empire* reported that over 30,000 workers had walked off their jobs in protest against bad working conditions and low wages. The conservative paper featured photographs of rampaging mobs facing mounted police and armed soldiers. Such scenes intensified the wish that international efforts could prevent labour outbreaks like this.

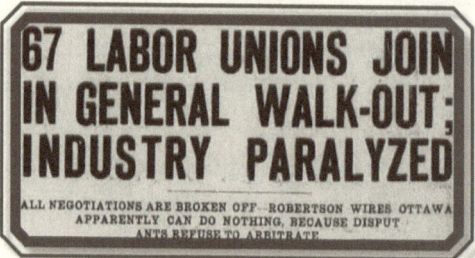

A major conference in Washington, D.C. in the fall of 1919 was planned, to begin setting worldwide standards on hours of work, minimum wages, night work for women, and minimum age for young workers. To the delight of everyone in Toronto, the Hon. Walter Riddell was selected to go to this conference as a Canadian delegate. Workers in his department would prepare materials for him to take to Washington. Zoë's thrill over this honour was contagious. All the Smiths became advocates for Riddell and for his vision of postwar labour conditions.

Zoë brought home rumours that Riddell's role in the early years of the international labour movement might expand. Whispers circulated that he and his staff might eventually move to Geneva if the League of Nations decided to back this part of its stated agenda.

Arthur and Lizzie were particularly pleased to hear Zoë's account of her research, though not particularly pleased to recognize a faint possibility that she might someday be offered a chance to go abroad following Mr. Riddell's leadership. Zoë's father had long cherished an unspoken hope that she might someday find a place in the Canadian Pacific organization. His old company was already offering employment to many young people, mostly men of course, and mostly veterans of the years of overseas war. But there should be room for some of the newly ambitious young women who had joined the workforce during the war.

At least Arthur's friend Dan would soon be back in Canada and settled in line for a postwar job at the Canadian Pacific. In early fall, word came that he and Colonel Ramsey had been ordered to England for the ceremonial decommissioning of the Canadian Overseas Railway Construction Corps. The two comrades toured the London theatres and visited Savile Row tailors to order civilian clothes, and then sailed for home. Dan now wrote that Colonel Ramsey, believing that the stresses of war had left him unable to serve effectively as CPR's Chief Construction Engineer, had convinced the Company to consider Dan as his possible successor.

After a brief time in a Montreal military hospital for treatment of old shrapnel wounds, Dan was officially demobilized. The CPR assigned him a temporary desk in the engineering department at Windsor Station and gave him an overview of the work that awaited him in maintenance and construction.

His new superior officers told him that attention was urgently needed at many trouble spots ignored during the war. A map posted over his new desk suggested the extent of company expansion out west. Postwar immigration was putting a strain on tracks and bridges all across the continent.

As Acting Chief Construction Engineer in Montreal, Dan could not promise himself an early trip to Ontario, no matter how eager he was to visit his parents in Clachan and the Smiths in Toronto. He wrote to Bertha that he could only hope that she felt something akin to his frustration and eagerness for a meeting.

Meanwhile, Arthur was happily involved this fall in a local labour experiment. On a tour of the freight yards south of the Union Station, he and his maintenance director watched a hand-picked team of workers as they followed a time-checked routine for replacing damaged ties with new ones. These men had developed a rhythm of loosening plates, lifting rails, hauling out rotted wood, heaving in the new ties and refastening the rails on them.  Superintendent Smith agreed with his maintenance officer that this team was ready to move into the passenger train area. Particular sections of track could be temporarily barred there, while rerouted trains passed by.

Someday, Arthur hoped, machines would be developed to hoist the lines of track, swing new crossties into place, and let the trains roll on. For now, he was grateful to have the right men on the manual job. In general, labourers seemed happy in the renewal of the kind of work that had been suspended for five years of wartime restrictions. Arthur had no fear of recurrences of the kind of labour troubles he had faced in Montreal, back in 1908.

He thought happily about Dan, who would probably soon organize labourers on a grander scale once he was permanently installed as chief construction engineer of the giant railway system. A welcome letter announced that Dan now had well-earned permission to go to his family's home farm near Clachan for a pre-Christmas visit, and that he intended to return to Montreal by way of Toronto and a brief drop in at the Smiths' home.

On a November afternoon, Arthur joyfully welcomed his old friend at the Union Station. But Dan interjected, eagerly, "I must warn you that I am specially anxious to see Bertha again. She has been a marvellous correspondent all the time I was at the Front."

Arthur's smile was benign. "Yes, you two have kept the letters flowing. Indeed, she has carried on a wonderful correspondence with a number of soldiers. Her idea of war work, I suppose." He shifted quickly to what seemed more important to him. Lizzie wanted to offer a simple supper rather than dinner, so Dan could catch the 7:30 train back to Montreal. "Let's get a move on!"

For Arthur it was a genuine pleasure to welcome his friend to his Toronto house. He had been reminded by Lizzie not to monopolize the visitor, but forgot these instructions and lingered, chatting, when Lizzie and Zoë left the room to make final preparations for dinner. Lizzie quickly returned to ask Arthur for help in moving the extra dining room chairs.

Bertha at last felt free to look directly at her visitor. The black hair she remembered was gray now, after five years of war. But the hazel eyes were still intense and bright. She moved toward the fireplace, reached her hand up to rest on the mantel, and pointed toward the little Venetian mosaic propped up there. "Doves, and a golden bowl," Bertha said. Dan reached up to cover her hand with his.

The dining room doors opened and there was Zoë, saying, "Supper's on the table." Dan turned away from Zoë and spoke softly but urgently to Bertha. "I'll come back to Toronto as soon as I can. But I can't wait till then to talk about our future."

Zoë was clearing her throat. "We're very short of time," she reminded them. There was no choice but to follow her into the dining room and join the family for a hurried supper. By the time she served dessert, Zoë had already telephoned for a taxi to come and take Dan to the Union Station in time for the evening train. There was no more private talk until the moment before Dan left, to return to Montreal.

Arthur stepped out to see whether the taxi had arrived. Lizzie tactfully hustled Zoë out of the room. Not much time for talk, after five years of wanting with increasing intensity to see each other. Dan quickly took her hand in his again. "I came today because I wanted to ask you to marry me. If I had time to ask, would you say yes?"

What was the point of appearing prim and proper? She looked straight at him and answered. "Yes, I would." Then she hurried to add that they must make sure her father wasn't hurt at being kept in the dark about this sudden turn.

Arthur filled the taxi ride with good-humoured gossip. But sitting in the Montreal train as it left the station, Dan began to write a note to him, about his continuing friendship and admiration for Arthur, and his eagerness to maintain that relationship. Then he wrote simply about his growing love for Bertha and asked for Arthur's agreement to their marriage.

Arthur turned out to be less bemused than expected. He quickly perceived how little he had understood the undercurrents. "Delighted," he wrote the day Dan's letter arrived, and he meant it. He thought happily how much he had enjoyed the brief first visit; other happy thoughts followed, to be shared with his family, about the future.

Zoë thought rather ruefully that romance like Bertha's didn't seem to be catching. She was now twenty-four years old. "If it takes five years for me to find the right man, like Bertha, I will be twenty-nine. Old, like Bertha!"

Back at work in Montreal Dan could write in a similar vein, "I'm over forty now, and I don't want to waste any more time. How soon can we count on being married?" They set a date: in early August in the coming year.

twenty-three

Concourse
High Park, 1920

In Montreal, well-wishers dropped into Dan's office to congratulate him when a notice of his engagement appeared in the Montreal *Gazette*. D.C. Coleman, the Vice-President rumoured to be in line for the presidency some day, proclaimed he was delighted to learn that Dan was to marry the daughter of his old friend "A.L." Like Arthur, Dan in his office in Windsor Station was doubly glad that he too no longer faced shortages in ties or rails or manpower. He was absorbed in planning for new tunnels and bridges, particularly out west  to aid postwar settlement. On a rare day off, he used nearly all his five years' war service savings to buy an upright piano, to be delivered in August to his semi-furnished apartment on Prud'homme Street.

For Arthur Lloyd Smith, Superintendent of the Toronto Railways Terminal, his morning glance into the Union Station concourse provided increasing satisfaction. The light-coloured walls were still rising, day by day, to their planned height, up to the two-storey-high vaulted ceiling, now being faced with sound-absorbing terracotta tiles, less than an inch thick, set in thin layers of cement.

Before the war began, the Montreal architectural firm of Ross & Macdonald had collaborated with CPR designers, Hugh Jones of Montreal and John Lyle of Toronto, to produce brilliant designs for the station. International praise had been lavished on their concepts. There were no worries about the beauty as well as the efficiency of the proposed edifice. Yet the actual construction had progressed very slowly since 1915. That would change now, Arthur thought. Soon the architects would return to their drawing boards and submit to the Terminals Board their final designs for a decorative frieze to be set beneath that vaulted ceiling. Arthur had heard rumours about the possibilities. Maybe heraldic designs, painted shields displaying the emblems of each of the provinces? Or an ornamental script emblazoned with the names of the major Canadian cities served by the railways? For the CPR, the list could easily be compiled, in Arthur's opinion, reading from east to west, as the trains came toward Toronto and the moved on: *Saint John · Fredericton · Quebec · Montreal · Toronto · Hamilton · Windsor · Sault Ste. Marie · Sudbury · Fort William · Regina · Moose Jaw · Calgary · Vancouver.* A few years ago, Arthur would have been hard-pressed to rattle off a second list of such dominant names, when innumerable independent lines criss-crossed the country. In July, 1920, however, all this complex of old lines had been officially renamed the "Canadian National Railway." So Arthur could now imagine a CNR list of central stations in the approach to Toronto, running this time from west to east, sea to sea, strung out slightly north of the CPR line: *Prince Rupert · Edmonton · Saskatoon · Winnipeg · Port Arthur · North Bay · Sarnia · London · Toronto · Ottawa · Sherbrooke · Lévis · Moncton · Halifax · Charlottetown.*

Such lists would mark the emergence of an uneasy peace in the railway world. When the Union Station, in all its glory, finally opened to the public, it would also stand as a testimonial to all the people who had constructed and maintained and managed the lines that tied the country together. Arthur Smith looked forward confidently to that day.

Until that happened, however, he and all the other station workers had to enter by a side door, and forge a way to the train sheds via a rickety bridge. He must bring his thoughts down from the

soaring dome of the concourse to the practical problems visible at the platform level. Trains rumbling to a stop; trains slowly chugging into motion: a picture to remember.

Regrettably, there were different rumblings and chuggings in the Toronto newspapers nowadays about possible troubles to come. These were political problems. The Toronto City Council threatened to face off against the railways over the question of traffic crossings. Would the city traffic continue to roll down to the waterfront, crossing on the same level as the huge and growing stretch of railway tracks? Or would the city agree to build underpasses to separate once and for all the burgeoning city street traffic?

Arthur remembered the amicable decisions reached by the city councillors and the railways' management in his early days at Parkdale. The underpass choice came easily at that time, and the actual construction turned out to be swift and congenial. Maybe those good old days would be repeated here at the Union Station. But this modern negotiation was on a larger scale, and with much more complicated sensitivities to be soothed. It might take a lot of time.

Untroubled by Toronto's political storm clouds, Dan and Bertha moved quietly through the summer months. In June, he arranged to take Bertha to his parents' farm in southwestern Ontario, so that they would not feel like strangers when August came around. The gentle elderly parents were delighted that their son, much too long a bachelor, had at last found a quiet young woman, "pretty as a picture." Two of Dan's sisters, Nancy and Maggie Belle, came to visit, establishing more new family ties.

Back in Toronto for the Dominion Day holiday, Dan and Bertha straightened out wedding plans. The essential fact was that neither he nor Bertha wanted the fuss of a formal church wedding. Zoë reacted to this idea in high management style.

Cousin Gertrude's fiancé could officiate in a service here at home, she declared. The Reverend Archibald Tuer was a Presbyterian minister, and that would please Dan's parents, who held a Protestant horror of pageantry and ritual. Zoë would ask John Sargent, the organist at Church of the Epiphany, to play the piano during the service. Furthermore, Zoë would produce a wedding luncheon here at home. As for a wedding cake, she would find a library book on how to decorate—something elegant.

Dan, rather daunted by this managerial display, whisked Bertha away on a quiet walk. This was to be her wedding, he reassured her, and Zoë must be made to leave decisions to her. Dan and Bertha wandered through High Park toward Grenadier Pond, where the legend of lost soldiers lingered, disturbing to a recent soldier. Dan felt that he too had drowned in some ways in the five-year pond of war. For Bertha, the shining pond was a reminder of sunny days on McGregor Bay with young Jim Laing, but the memory came with no regrets. Dan was the man for her and there would be a smooth passage through to the wedding in August.

But that is not the way life is. Zoë came home from work in July, in an exalted mood. She burst out as the family sat down for dinner with "the most marvellous news!" and explained that Mr. Riddell was now choosing the team he would take to Geneva—"And he wants me to be part of it!" She noted with delight that the team would not be leaving until three days after Bertha's wedding. "Isn't that great?" She caught her breath. "I will have to get some new clothes. And a passport. So much to do!"

"But Zoë –" Bertha and Arthur both spoke at once. Then Arthur took a deep breath and spoke alone, very seriously. "But we will need you more than ever after Bertha leaves. Your mother simply can't manage alone."

Lizzie stopped him. "Zoë must have her chance."

"Not if it means your health, Mother."

Zoë was rendered speechless. Temporarily. Then she began to argue, and her arguments were fierce and heartfelt and logical. Bertha could stay home a little longer. Why was Bertha's marriage more important that Zoë's chance for an international career? To be in Geneva watching Mr. Riddell help make historic decisions on international standards! Fixing the future in labour regulations! Contributing to the inauguration of the new League of Nations—didn't that outweigh Bertha's desire to be married so soon?

"Soon?" Bertha cried. "After five years of waiting?" while Lizzie whispered, "Dears! Dears!" her breath coming in short gasps. She wasn't strong enough to speak.

Arthur made a pronouncement, "An unmarried daughter's place is with her mother."

In the short run at least, Lizzie's needs trumped the League of Nations. Zoë would stay home.

"Maybe there will be another chance to join Mr. Riddell?" Bertha asked her in private.

"Not likely. And who's to say Mother's heart won't kick up again just at the crucial moment?" Nevertheless, in the whirl of arrangements for the wedding Zoë almost forgot her bitter disappointment.

Dan, coming back to Toronto on the overnight train on the eighth of August, found Arthur waiting on the platform. The two men proceeded together up the ramp to the central block, still in the nearly final stage. As they walked through the holiday crowds on the ramp, Arthur was constantly greeted cheerfully by the workers: redcap porters, baggage handlers, clerks, and other office personnel. Dan, delighted to feel the warmth and respect directed toward his old friend, passed along greetings from the range of Montreal acquaintances. Across the postwar country, hopefulness, energy, and loyalty tied the CPR veterans together.

Wedding gifts arrived at Geoffrey Street. Among others, Jack and Eola sent a painting by Tom Thomson, "one of the young fellows who are showing the real look of the country north of Superior." They also sent regrets: they had to fly out to Flin Flon that week to check up on a major investment. Another gift came from Harry McLean, who had recently announced his engagement to a young lady in Westmount. He sent a handsome set of leather-bound books on Canadian history, sporting the bookplate image of a winged horse, set against the wheels of a modern locomotive.

It was a quiet wedding at home, in deference to Dan's non-conformist parents. But organist John Sargent heralded Bertha with a touch of pomp as she came down the stairs and into the living room with her father. Dan, shaking a little, turned to welcome his bride, while his parents smiled in gentle pleasure and joined in singing the old-time children's hymn, "All things bright and beautiful." Cousin Gertrude's husband, the Reverend Archie, pronounced the ceremonial phrases with warmth and dignity.

When the service ended, Dan and Bertha, the two sets of parents, and the minister—and Grandmother Smith, who had announced she was ignoring the note about a "private ceremony"—signed the official registry, while Mr. Sargent played a Handel aria and quietly sang the words:

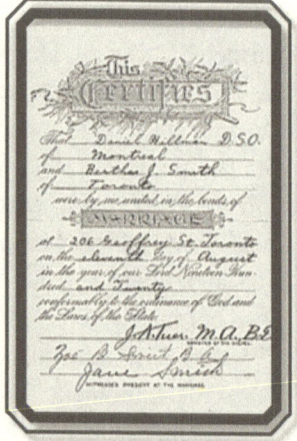

> *Where'er you walk, cool gales shall fan the glade;*
>
> *Trees, where you sit, shall crowd into a shade.*
>
> *Where'er you tread, the blushing flowers shall rise . . .*

All very pretty, Dan thought; and his mind flashed to bombed-out parks in Belgium. But he had had enough of realism for five horrible years. Time for illusions now, at least for a while.

Then Zoë called everyone out to the garden for picture-taking. The organist took photographs of the family group, including Dan's parents, on the left, and Grandmother Smith, on the far right. The Reverend Archie and Arthur and Gertrude stood behind the group. So did Zoë, peeking over her mother's shoulder. Lizzie stood front and centre with the bridal couple.

Then Zoë cried, "Time for lunch!" and led the way through to the dining room, where the table bore as its glorious climax the wedding cake she had created.

Finally, everyone set out to the Union Station to see the new couple catch the train for Montreal, where they would board a tour ship bound for a Bermuda honeymoon. Arthur led the little group back through the station to Front Street, and sent them to Geoffrey Street in munificent taxicabs.

So the story ends as it began, with a marriage—and both would last many years.

Once back in her own home when the guests left, Lizzie began to straighten up the house. She paused to dust the little Venetian mosaic: "Birds in their little nest," as she remembered saying to her daughters. Now one bird had flown, and the other was dipping her wings in the dangerous waters of "Rights for Women." Lizzie sighed, then went back to the kitchen for a lonely cup of tea.

Arthur had gone back to work. He moved past the concourse of the Union Station, still a bit of a shambles, but a loving eye could envision the glory of its eventual completion. He liked the word "concourse"; he had looked it up in his old dictionary and found it meant not only the place where people assembled, but also the act of coming together. Then he rode the old, soon-to-be-replaced elevator up to his office. Not a grand place as yet, but the architect's sketches for the office level included a suite for the Superintendent, with his own bathroom and a separate anteroom for his private secretary.

He stole another glance at the designs. In the arrivals area there would be paintings featuring each of the Canadian provinces—enough to excite and delight Canadian travellers. All the provinces would be brought together by the railway, with freight trains linking their diverse commercial interests, and passenger trains tying families into cross-country closeness. Visitors would go by train to see vistas of Rocky Mountain grandeur or vignettes of Quebec City, to revel in the prairie expanses, or to savour a whiff of the bracing air in the Maritimes. The Toronto Union Station would pound with energy—like the heart of 1920s Canada.

Afterword

This book owes a lot to my family—parents, son and four daughters and their spouses, plus ten adult grandchildren—who aid and abet my devotion to research, writing, and railways. My winter writers' group encouraged the first scribblings on railroad rivalries and sisterhood. Jim Lyons, perceptive and patient editor, polished the consequent manuscript. Railway historian Charles Cooper checked and corrected details about construction and maintenance, and endorsed use of photos from his collection. Blessed Jen Rubio, working with Rock's Mills Press, framed the illustrations and fitted them into an elegant publication. My "other family"—longtime friends and colleagues including Mary Rubio, Betsy Epperly, Catherine Ross and Penn Kemp—still sustain my adventures in writerland.

—Elizabeth Waterston, MC, OOnt, FRSC,
Professor Emerita, University of Guelph.

This story is based primarily on photographs, journals, letters, and official documents currently held by the Baldwin, Smith, and Hillman families: a family archive indicated in the following list as "FA." Additional illustrations come from local, business and national archives, as noted in the paginated list: I gratefully acknowledge the courtesy of the people at these repositories who granted permission to reproduce illustrations in their collections. Photographs of railway equipment come from *Wikipedia*, photographs of stations and construction sites from the Charles Cooper collection and specialized websites such as *Canada Rail* and *Old Time Trains*. I thank the many historians including Derek Boles and Dale Wilson who answered my questions about material in old websites that no longer appear on the web. Some of these defunct sites have been subsumed by "exporail.com."

Illustrations and their sources, listed by pages on which they appear.

1 Elizabeth Baldwin. Family Archive (FA); **2** Arthur Smith. FA; Smith family. FA; **3** OS&HR Engine. Toronto Public Library. Special Collections (TPL); **4** Aurora GTR station. Aurora Museum and Archives (AMA); Telegraph key. Canadian Historical Railway Association website (CHRA); **5** "Messages Sent": FA; **6** Settee: FA; **8** Ingersoll CPR station: Oxford County Resource Centre (OCRC); Commemorative arch: Library and Archives Canada (LAC); **9** Lizzie: FA; **10** GTR station: Charles Cooper's Railway Pages (CCRP); **11** Railway switch: Wikipedia (W); Giant Cheese: Ingersoll Cheese and Agricultural Museum ; **12** Lincoln Smith: FA; North Parkdale GTR Station: CCRP; **15** Junction: West Toronto Junction Historical Society; Weston Station: Weston Historical Society (WHS); **16** Trains at Junction: TPL; **17** Sorting yard diagram. *Journal of Transport Literature*; Link-and-pin: W; Shunting engine: CP Corporate Archive (CPCA); **18** Bertha Jane: F; **19** Janney coupler: W; Buffer: W; **21** Grandma Baldwin: FA; **22** Woodbridge Station: City of Vaughan Archive; Mixed Gauge: Paris Museum and Historical Society (PMHS); **23** Workers changing gauges. Uxbridge-Scott Museum (USM); Hand switches: W; **24** Lizzie with Bertha: FA; **25** Lizzie with Gertrude Baldwin: FA; **26** Anah: FA; **27** Bertha: FA; **28** Parkdale Station: CCRP; Map of Cowan Street: W; **29** House on Cowan Street: TPL; **30** Queen Street underpass: City of Toronto Archive, (CTA); **31** Grandmother Jane Smith: FA; Lizzie, Zoë and Bertha Smith: FA. **33** Girl with muff: FA; **35** Islington Station: CCRP; Emery Station: CCRP; West Toronto Station: CCRP; **36** Victoria Public School: CTA; Happy family: FA; Completed overpass: CTA; **38** Anah's plate: FA; **39** White River: White River Heritage Museum (WHRM); **40** White River Village: WHRM; White River Station: WHRM; **42** Harry McLean: FA; **43** Lizzie and Zoë: FA; Notice board: FA; **44** Handcart: LAC; **45** Tunnel: W; Daniel Hillman: FA; **46** Anah: FA; Walker Hotel: TPL; **47** St. Mark's Church: TPL; Clock: FA; **48** 1902 style: FA; North Toronto Station: CCRP; Railway timetable: (LAC); **49** Don Station; CCRP; **50** Parkdale Collegiate

Institute: TPL; **52** Parkdale Collegiate pin: FA; Toronto fire, 1904: TPL; **53** Mimico yards: LAC; **55** London CPR station: CCRP; Railway signals: W; **56** Talbot Street: London Public Library, Ivey Family Room (LPL); London Grand Trunk Railway Station: LPL; **57** Carling Brewery: LPL; **58** Tea time style: FA; **59** Shopping: FA; Victorian chair: FA; **60** GTR map: W; Bertha at age 15: FA; **61** D.C. Coleman: CPCA; **65** Bertha at 16. FA; Eola Jaffray: FA; **66** Mearle Gordon: FA; **67** Bertha and Eola: FA; Motorcar: FA; **68** Girls on bridge: FA; **69** Tea party: FA; **70** Tadoussac Hotel: CPCA; **71** CPR Windsor Station: CPCA; Angus Shops: CPCA; **73** Montreal lookout: Westmount Public Library (WPL); Fashion: FA; **74** *Golden Gleams of Thought*: FA; **75** Trinity College, Toronto: Trinity College Archives (TCA); Class of '12: FA; **76** Zoë and Dora: FA; **77** Viger Station: CPCA; **78** Westmount house: FA; Bûche de Noël: W; **80** Train Wreck: CPCA; News clip: FA; **81** Map of Farnham: W; **82** Farnham station: Eastern Townships Resource Centre (ETRC); Buffy and friends: FA; **83** Megantic: FA; Arthur and Zoë: FA; A.L. Smith: FA; **84** C.M. Hays: W; **85** Bertha and Bea: FA; Zoë at 16: FA; Grandmother Smith: FA; Grandpa Baldwin: FA; **86** Votes for Women: FA; **87** Daunting countryside: FA; **88** Spur: FA; Sudbury CPR station: CPCA; Sudbury house: FA; **89** Dan FA; **91** Arthur Lloyd Smith: FA; Work team: FA; **92** Bertha and Jim: FA; Zoë with tub: FA; **94** McGill class of 1915: FA; Sudbury downtown: Greater Sudbury Library (GSL); **97** Zoë, YMCA: FA; C.M Hays: W; **98** Kenora Tourist Hotel: Lake of the Woods Museum (LWM); **99** Lake Superior map: (LWM); **102** German junction: W; Zoë at camp: FA; Bertha: FA; **104** Zoë in Muskoka: FA; New Sudbury station: GSL; Horse and buggy: FA; **105** Bertha and Jim: FA; Professor Stephen Leacock: FA; **107** Bertha and friends: FA; **108** CPR crossing: W; Wigwag: W; Telegraph building: GSL; **109** Zoë at Y camp: FA; Bertha and Eleanor Laing: FA; **110** Zoë on a rock: FA; **111** Jim and friends: FA; **112** Map: W; **113** Harry Beatty: FA; Marchers: FA; **116** CORCC: FA; **117** Zoë and Dora: FA; **118** Fishplates: W; **119** Tracks out west: W **120** Wartime Crowds: CTA; **121** Lizzie: FA; Arthur and Lizzie with Bertha: FA; Canoeing: FA; Toronto Normal School: TPL; **124** Lizzie and Bertha with hats: FA; Zoë at business school: FA; **125** Church of the Epiphany: TPL; Construction of Union Station: TPL; **126** Red Cross pins: FA; Crater: W; **128** Zoë: FA; **129** Edward Beatty: CPCA; **131**

Algoma locomotive: www.OldTimeTrains (OTT); **132** Pegasus: FA; Balmoral Hotel: GSL; **133** Map of AER: CHRA; **134** Knox College: TPL; **135** Zoë's hat: FA; Algoma Eastern engine: (OTT); Ready for rails: OTT; **136** ACR station: Sault Ste. Marie Public Library (SSMPL) CR; **137** Agawa trestle (SSMPL); 19.11, Agawa canyon: SSMPL; **138** Citation: FA; **141** Surviving officers: FA; original officers FA; DSO: FA; **142** Jack Hammell: FA; **43** Edward Beatty: CPCA; **144** D.C. Coleman: CPCA; **146** Dan Hillman: FA; **147** Doves: FA; **149** Brake man: W; **150** Brake system: W; **153** Union Station concourse: www.toronto transit (TT); Waiting room: TT; **154** North Toronto station: CCRP; **155** Rotting ties: W; **156** Walter Riddell: W; Winnipeg strike news: University of Manitoba Archives (UMA); Winnipeg strike crowd: UMA; **158** CPR map: CPCA; Replacing ties, W; **159** Doves: FA; **161** D.C. Coleman: CPCA; Union Station ceiling: TT; **162** Train sheds; TPL; **163** Zoë retreating: FA; **166** wedding certificate: FA; Wedding party: FA; wedding cake: FA; **167** Lizzie: FA; Arthur: FA.

Sources

For railway enthusiasts, I offer this selected list of useful items, old and new.

Boles, Derek. "Ontario, Simcoe & Huron Railway." *www.canada-rail.com*, 2011.

-----..*Toronto's Railway Heritage*. Toronto: Arcadian Publishing, 2000.

"Built-from-the-Rock." Flin Flon: Hudbay Minerals Inc., 2015.

Burnett, R.G. "Railway Telegraph and Telephone." *www.canada-rail.com*, 1991.

"British Army Asks for Corps of Canadian Railwaymen, 1915. CORCC Overseas, Wartime and Post-war." *www.canada-rail.com*, 1993.

Cooper, Charles. *Narrow Gauge for Us: The Story of the Toronto and Nipissing Railway*. Erin: Boston Mills Press, 1982.

-----. "Ontario Railway Stations." *www.railwaypages.com*, 2014.

Cruikshank, Ken. *Close Ties: Railways, Government, and the Board of Railway Commissioners, 1851–1933*. Montreal: McGill-Queen's University Press, 1991.

Cruise, David and Alison Griffiths. *Lords of the Line: The Men Who Built the CPR*. Markham: Penguin, 1988.

Currie, A.W. *The Grand Trunk Railway of Canada*. Toronto: University of Toronto Press, 1957.

Houston, Mary. *White River: 100 Years (1885–1995)*. White River: Houston, 1985.

Innis, Harold. *The Canadian Pacific Railway*. Toronto: McClelland & Stewart, 1923.

Kennedy, R.L. "Algoma Eastern Railway." *www.canada-rail.com*.

Kerr, Donald, "The Geography of the Canadian Iron-Steel Industry," *Economic Geography*, 335, 2, 1959.

Lamb, W.K. *History of the Canadian Pacific Railway*. N.Y.: Macmillan, 1977.

Mackinnon, Mary. "Trade Unions and Employment Stability at the Canadian Pacific Railway, 1903–29." *Origins of the Modern Career*, ed. David Mitch et al. Aldershot: Ashgate, 2004.

Marinov, Marin, et al. "Analysis of Rail Yard and Terminal Performances." *Journal of Transport Literature* (April 2014).

Marshall, Sean and James Bow. "A History of Toronto's Union Station Through the 19th and 20th Centuries." transit.toronto.on.ca. 2015.

Ontario Department of Crown Lands. *Report of the Survey and Exploration of Northern Ontario, 1900*. Toronto: Queen's Printer for Ontario, 1900.

Riff, Carl. "Train Wreck." *www.canada-rail.com*, 1991.

Rossiter, W.H. *The Canadian Pacific in Southern Ontario*. vols. 1–3. Calgary: W.H. Smith, 1980–86.

Rowe, Johanna. *Superior Tales and Trails*. amazon.com, 2012.

Wilson, Dale. *Algoma Eastern Railway*. Sudbury: Nickel Belt Rails, 1977.

------. "Algoma Central Railway, Bear-Watching Then and Now." *www.exporail.org/can_rail*, 1979.

------. "Algoma Eastern Railway: The Line to Little Current." *www.exporail.org_can_rail*, 1973.

www.ingramcontent.com/pod-product-compliance
Lightning Source LLC
Chambersburg PA
CBHW030908080526
44589CB00010B/195